RETURN
FROM
TOMORROW

RETURN FROM TOMORROW

GEORGE G. RITCHIE, M.D.

with Elizabeth Sherrill

Published by
chosen books

FLEMING H. REVELL COMPANY
OLD TAPPAN, NEW JERSEY

Library of Congress Cataloging in Publication Data

Ritchie, George G., M.D., 1923–
    Return from tomorrow.

        1. Ritchie, George G., M.D., 1923–   2. Christian biography—
United States.   3. Psychiatrists—United States–Biography.
4. Death, Apparent—Case studies.   I. Sherrill, Elizabeth,
joint author.   II. Title.
BR1725.R58A37   248'.2'0924[B]   77-27543
ISBN 0-8007-9067-7

A Chosen Book
Copyright © 1978 by George G. Ritchie, M.D.
Chosen Books are Published by
Fleming H. Revell Company
Old Tappan, New Jersey
Printed in the United States of America

To *His* three ladies

Marguerite Shell Ritchie who married not
only me but the experience which has
governed my life.

Catherine Marshall who first insisted I
tell it all.

Elizabeth Sherrill who helped me find
the words.

RETURN
FROM
TOMORROW

Foreword

Looking back at its history and development, philosophy might well be characterized as an obsession with death. Death has always been a deep and fundamental concern of philosophers. It is not so surprising then, that as a twenty-one year old undergraduate philosophy student I was intrigued when in 1965 I learned of a man who had undergone an apparent clinical "death," had had an incredible experience in the interim, and had lived to tell of it. Not only that, this man was a respected physician—at that time a resident psychiatrist with a fourteen-year career as a general practitioner already behind him—and he was willing to share his story with others. Needless to say, I availed myself of the opportunity to hear him speak, was profoundly impressed, and mentally "filed it away." Later, hearing other quite similar accounts, I began investigating near-death experiences.

The psychiatrist's name is George Ritchie, and now he has told his experience for publication: the chronicle of one of the three or four most fantastic and well-documented "dying" experiences known to me. Even in isolation, Dr. Ritchie's story is startling; it is perhaps even more so when one realizes that hundreds upon hundreds of other persons who have had close calls with death have come back with remarkably similar accounts.

The question will remain for many: "Was George Ritchie (and were the many others who have found themselves in such circumstances) really dead?" Admittedly, if one defines "death"—as seems eminently reasonable—as that state of the body from which restoration of function is impossible, then none of these people were dead. In the clinical sense, however, the whole matter of the final criteria for diagnosing death is very much up in the air just now, very much unsettled among the medical profession itself. For my own part, I am content to reflect that whatever state one understands final bodily death to be, Dr. Ritchie and others like him have come much, much closer to it than have the great majority of their living fellow human beings. For that reason alone, I for one am quite willing to listen to what they have to say.

Another question which frequently comes up with respect to these experiences is what kind of effect they have on the lives of those to whom they happen. As will be obvious from his account, Dr. Ritchie's experience has had an enormous—indeed central—effect on the life he leads. Unfortunately, only those of us who know him as a friend can truly sense the depth of kindness, understanding, and loving concern for others which characterize this remarkable man.

With those remarks, let me get out of the way and introduce you to my friend George. I hope that, through this book, you will come to know and love him as my family and I do.

DR. RAYMOND A. MOODY, JR.
Author, *Life After Life*

10

I

I got to my office early, as I liked to do, to have a few minutes alone before my first patient arrived. I glanced around the still-shaded room—the desk, the comfortable chairs, the yellow sofa in front of the window. I found the practice of psychiatry deeply satisfying. During the thirteen years I had worked as a medical doctor, I'd often had the sense that I was treating only parts of a person, dealing with symptoms of disease rather than the disease itself. At Memorial Hospital in Richmond, Virginia, where I had practiced, as at any large modern hospital, there was no time to know my patients as people. No time to listen to the questions behind the ones they asked in the consulting room.

So at age forty, I had gone back to school. It hadn't been easy to ask my wife to leave Richmond and move to

Charlottesville, to uproot our two children from school, to give up my position as president of the Richmond Academy of General Practice, and to go back for more years of study and residency. But in the dozen years since that decision, I had been glad of it many times, and never more so than in this quiet moment at the start of the day.

I flipped open the engagement pad on the desk and ran down the list of appointments for the day. Mildred Brown. Peter Jones. Jane Martin.* Then my finger stopped.

My first appointment after lunch was Fred Owen. I had forgotten that yesterday he was getting out of the University clinic. I'd had the report by phone last week from Fred's physician—"carcinoma of the lungs with metastasis to the brain"—but I had known already. Fred was dying of lung cancer. I had suspected it back in September, five months ago, when he first came to see me with symptoms of severe depression. The depression, the hacking cough, the chain smoking throughout our sessions, had all alerted me and I had made an appointment for him to have a complete physical examination at the University of Virginia Medical School hospital here in Charlottesville.

Apparently Fred never kept that appointment. Three weeks ago, growing suspicious again, I had examined him right here in this room. I didn't have proper equipment of course, but through a stethoscope I had heard enough. Since then he had been in the University Hospital undergoing a battery of tests and consultations. But this had been more for Fred's sake than because there was any doubt in the matter.

And now, at 1:00 this afternoon, he would be here. How could I help him face the tremendous fact of his own death?

---

* Patients' names have been changed.

He had made such enormous strides in the months he had been coming here, but he had such a long way still to go. Time was what he desperately needed. And time was what Fred no longer had.

Furthermore this inoperable cancer coming right now—he was only in his mid-forties—would seem to him the very negation of all the gains he had made. To him it would prove exactly what his neurosis had always claimed: that the world and everyone in it had conspired against him since the time he was born. The trouble was, he wasn't altogether wrong. From a mother who had neglected him, through a series of unstable foster homes, to a succession of bosses who had exploited him, and a disastrous marriage, he had known little but sick relationships. Developing healthier ones had been our goal. Starting with the beginnings of trust in me he had been reaching out for the first time in his life for real friendships. And now he was dying! The ultimate betrayal had happened, the final proof that the game had been rigged against him from the start.

Between other appointments that morning my mind kept turning to Fred. At lunchtime I had a sandwich sent in and ate at my desk in case he arrived early. But 1:00 P.M. came, and 1:15, and no sign of Fred. He arrived at 1:35, the first time in five months he had been late for his session.

"I won't be able to pay you," he said even before sitting down. "I quit work this morning. Told those tight-fisted so-and-so's exactly what I thought of them! They wanted me to stay until they could find a replacement, but why should I do anything for them?

"Four months the doctors give me!" he went on, flinging himself into the armchair with what was probably meant to sound like a laugh. "What a joke, huh doc? All this digging around in the past so I can do better in the future—only now I'm not going to have a future! Work things through with my mother, work things through with my wife—all a waste of time now, huh?"

"On the contrary," I told him. "These things are more urgent now than they've ever been. Your future depends more than you can guess on how swiftly you get on with this business of relationships."

He stared at me, his wounded eyes terrible to see. "My future?" he echoed. "I just told you they give me four months, which probably means four weeks, because doctors lie like everyone else. Frankly, I don't think it's worth the trouble."

"I'm not talking about four months or four weeks or forty years. I'm talking about the future that has no measurement."

Like a door slammed in my face I saw the openness go out of his eyes. "Are you talking about . . . heaven and hell, that sort of thing? Come off it, doc!"

He was trying to keep up his devil-may-care tone, but I could see that I had made him angry. Our relationship had been built up, slowly over the weeks, on the understanding that I would "play it straight" with him. This was all-important; he often commented that I was the first person who had never tried to deceive him.

"I never thought I'd get that from you, of all people! If I wanted to hear a lot of mumbo-jumbo about death not being the end, I'd have gone to some pie-in-the-sky minister. They'll promise you wings and a harp and anything else you want, if you drop a big enough bill in the plate."

I took a deep breath, groping for the right words—or at

least not the wrong ones. I knew enough of Fred's early history to know that anything that even hinted of religion was anathema to him. The cruelest of the three sets of foster parents with whom he had lived had been a pious church-going couple who believed they could beat the sullenness out of the withdrawn little boy.

"I don't know anything about harps and wings," I said. "I can only tell you what I myself observed after—"

I paused, fearful of the perilous word that might undo the bridge of trust erected between us. "After I died"—that's what I had started to say. But here was a man who had often been lied to. How could I share this turning point of my life with him, without sounding like the biggest liar of all?

"Fred," I began hesitantly, "doctors gave up on me one time, too. I was pronounced dead—sheet pulled up over my head. The fact that after ten minutes or so I was brought back to live a while longer on this earth is to me just a parenthesis in a much bigger story. It's that big story, Fred, that I'd like to tell you about."

Fred took out a pack of cigarettes and lit one with a hand that trembled. "You're asking me to believe that you got a look into some kind of future life? That's what you're going to say isn't it—it doesn't matter if this life's a lousy cheat because everything's coming up roses in the next?"

"I'm not asking you to believe anything. I'm simply telling you what I believe. And I have no idea what the next life will be like. Whatever I saw was only—from the doorway, so to speak. But it was enough to convince me totally of two things from that moment on. One, that our consciousness does not cease with physical death—that it becomes in fact keener and more aware than ever. And secondly, that how we spend our time on earth, the kind of relationships we build, is vastly, infinitely more important than we can know."

For several minutes Fred had been too angry at me to look me in the face. "If you were as sick as you claim," he asked, eyes on the brown-and-green carpet, "how do you know you weren't delirious?"

"Because, Fred, this experience was the most entirely real thing that's ever happened to me. Since that time, too, I've had a chance to study dreams and hallucinations. I've had patients who were hallucinating. There's just no resemblance."

"You mean you honestly believe we go on . . . being ourselves? Afterwards, I mean?"

"I've bet my life on it. Everything I've done in the last thirty years—becoming a doctor, becoming a psychiatrist, all the hours of volunteer work with young people each week—all of it goes back to that experience. I don't believe delirium could do that, govern a man's entire life."

"Delirium couldn't," he agreed. "But what if it wasn't just a momentary delusion? What if you've been, you know, off base all along?"

"What if I'm crazy, you mean?" I was smiling but the question was a legitimate one. The insane, of all mortals, seem the most plausible to themselves.

"That's a tough one to answer, Fred. I don't guess any of us can ever be sure we are making sense. I have one reason for hoping I am, anyway, and that's the grilling they put me through here at the University of Virginia before I could start training as a psychiatrist. I had to face every senior member of the staff, one by one, answer every kind of question they could put to me.

16

"Because the experience I'd had—the experience of death and what happened afterward—was so central to everything I believed, I felt they had a right to hear about it, so I told them. What the eminent doctors made of it I don't know, but after hearing me out, every one of them judged me both sane and emotionally stable."

"Which proves doctors are crazy," Fred said, but he was smiling, the first smile since he had come in, and I knew that whatever his reservations, at least he was ready to listen.

The story was too long to tell in one session or even in two, but I felt it would be worth however much time we spent at it. Fred being the kind of person he was, I knew better than to start with my personal interpretation. He would need to hear it detail by detail, exactly as it happened, then form his own opinion. "I'm not going to try to draw any conclusions, Fred. I'm just going to describe what happened, step by step, from the moment I entered that Army hospital. Later, if you want to talk about what it means—to me, to you—we can do that."

"Army hospital?" Fred asked. He counted back: "This was during the Second World War, wasn't it? You mean . . . you got shot?"

"It was during the war, but it wasn't a bullet that got me." I grinned ruefully, remembering. "It was the weather in west Texas. . . ."

II

I closed my eyes, remembering back thirty-four years, remembering the long train ride from Virginia out to Abilene, Texas, hundreds of us young recruits, many, like me, leaving home for the first time. I had been born and raised in Richmond, and I recalled my amazement that there was any place on earth where there weren't a lot of trees.

"It was the end of September, 1943," I began, "and I was on my way out to Camp Barkeley, Texas, for basic training." I was 20 years old, tall, skinny, a pretty typical kid of those days, full of idealism about winning the war and whipping the Nazis.

The only thing I hadn't been prepared to fight was dust. At the train station in Abilene we had been loaded onto trucks for the drive to camp, several miles out, and the dust was blowing so hard we never saw a thing the whole way. I knew Camp Barkeley had to be a huge place—there were supposed to be 250,000 men in training there—but it was days before the dust settled enough for me to get a look at it: a sprawling city of wooden barracks stretching into the desert.

During dust storms we had to drill wearing goggles, and even then we had to keep one hand on the shoulder of the guy ahead or we'd bump into each other. Then in November the rain began, and all that dust turned to mud. But the wind would dry off the surface and blow it in your face. They used to say it was the only place on earth where you could march in mud up to your knees and still get dust in your eyes.

In December, on top of everything else, it turned bitterly cold, colder than it ever got back in Richmond. On December 10 we sat on the ground—it was 10° above zero—for two hours while some young lieutenant lectured us on the proper way to clean equipment. That night our whole platoon was coughing.

Next morning my throat was still hurting, so I checked in at sick bay. Sure enough, I was running a fever, not very high, around 102°, but a jeep came and drove me over to the base hospital.

The hospital was an enormous five thousand-bed affair, occupying more than two hundred low wooden buildings all joined together with connecting walkways. Since I had a fever, the admitting nurse assigned me to an isolation ward. This was a twenty-four-bed barracks, with a doctor's office, a nurse's office, and a supply room on one side as you came in, and on the other side three little cubicles with a single bed in each one where they put you if you were really sick.

19

But all I had was that slight fever, so of course I was in the main ward beyond.

The only thing that worried me at all, in fact, was that it was now December 11, and on December 18 I had to be on a train, headed back for Virginia. I had just gotten the greatest break a twenty-year-old buck private had ever gotten from the U.S. Army, and I wasn't going to be cheated out of it by a stupid cold. On December 22 I was going to start classes at the Medical College of Virginia, in my hometown of Richmond, to become a doctor under the Army Specialized Training Program.

The amazement of it still had me waking up at night wondering if it were really true. It had been just after Thanksgiving when I was suddenly called in off the drill field to face a roomful of majors and colonels—even a couple of brigadier generals. I was sure it was a court-martial and was trying to recall from movies whether they gave you a chance to phone your parents or just took you out and shot you.

I stood at attention with my knees knocking while they fired questions at me. Was it true I had completed pre-med training at the University of Richmond? Was it true I had been accepted for entrance at the Medical College of Virginia? What had been my reason for enlisting in the Army instead, when medical students were automatically deferred?

At last one of the officers explained. By now, the winter of 1943, the Army was desperately short of doctors. Some time next year, everybody knew, the great Allied invasion of Europe would take place. How long after that would the war last? Five years? Six? They needed doctors fast, and obviously the quickest way to create them was to locate soldiers who had any kind of previous training.

Yes, I told them, quaking with relief, I had finished my pre-med the previous summer, at nineteen, doing the four-year course in two, as many were doing during the war. And yes, my application had been accepted at the Medical College of Virginia. As for why I had enlisted in the Army instead . . . it was kind of personal, but all these officers were looking at me, waiting for an answer.

It was on account of my dad, I told them, on account of his going into the service. They kept staring at me, waiting for the whole story, so I plunged in. My dad, I explained, was a coal expert with the C&O Railroad, traveling around to their big coal customers, showing them how to build efficient furnaces and so on. When the war came, the C&O loaned dad to the federal government, and he went all over the country inspecting coal-burning power plants at military bases. Then when the invasion of Europe became a possibility, he was given a commission in the Army and assigned to a group stockpiling fuel for D-Day.

Here was my father, well past normal draft age, ready to go overseas, and follow the first troops onto the Continent to set up fuel depots there. And here I was, age twenty, still going to school as though nothing had happened. So I had volunteered—and got sent to Camp Barkeley, Texas.

I didn't say this to the officers, of course, but a few weeks in the dust and mud had changed my mind about how much a foot soldier was worth in this war. And then, just as I was feeling that I counted for exactly nothing, came the incredible news that I was going to go to med school anyway, and the Army was going to send me!

I lay staring up at the wooden ceiling of the isolation ward in the baggy white pajamas they gave you, feeling pretty satisfied with the way things worked. I suppose if I had been a religious person I would have said God did it, but that didn't occur to me. Sure I'd gone to church, back home, but it hadn't been that important to me.

What was important was scouting. I had been a Boy Scout since I was twelve, working up from Tenderfoot all the way to Eagle and then, last summer, junior assistant Scout Master. So I naturally tended to think in terms of credits—points and promotions and that sort of thing. And now it was almost as though volunteering for the Army was a credit mark—a kind of good deed—and getting sent to med school the reward.

That was how life worked. Take medicine for example. All my life I had wanted to be a doctor, long before I was old enough to think about earning a living. Then in college I found out that while doing good for people doctors could also make a lot of money. The point was, you didn't go into it for the rewards. The rewards came as a result of doing the right thing.

The Army nurse stopped at my bed and shook down a thermometer. I put it under my tongue hoping at last there would be good news. It was now December 15; I had been in this ward four days with no improvement, and I was getting really worried about being aboard that train on the 18th. Even after the fever was gone, I knew, they kept you in a recuperation ward a couple of days.

She read the thermometer and marked her chart. "Still 102° I'm afraid," she said, sounding really sorry. I had told her about the great break I was getting and she and the rest of the staff seemed genuinely concerned.

I had pestered them until they rounded up a bunch of train schedules which I kept on the bedside table along with the water jug and drinking glass, the sputum cup and the night light. Among all this hospital paraphernalia those schedules were my link to the world outside. If by bad luck I was still here on the 18th, I would study every train route between here and Virginia till I found a way to be in Richmond for the start of classes on the 22nd. If I didn't show up, I knew there were a dozen other soldiers waiting to take my place. Even if by some miracle they held it for me, if I arrived after the rest of the class had started, my chances of catching up would be about nil. This was one of the most competitive programs in the service; I had been warned that a third of the class flunked out in the first nine months.

I swallowed the pill the nurse had left in a paper cup and returned to my comforting philosophy. I knew exactly why I had originally wanted to be a doctor. It wasn't for money. It was to help Papa Dabney.

Papa Dabney was my mother's father; I could close my eyes and see his blue eyes and bristling white moustache. The Dabneys were French Huguenots who had settled in Virginia in the eighteenth century, in a region which still retains its special speech. Papa Dabney's garden was always a "gyarden," his automobile a "cyah."

He and Mama Dabney were more like parents than grandparents to my older sister and me. A month after I was born our mother died, and Dad's work with the C&O meant that he traveled a lot. So Papa and Mama Dabney took Mary Jane and me to "Moss Side," their large old frame house on what was then the outskirts of Richmond.

It was a wonderful place for a small boy to grow up in. There were huge wicker chairs on the broad verandah, ancient live oaks in the yard. Until a city ordinance stopped her, Mama Dabney kept a cow and chickens on the lawn. She was an old-fashioned little lady who called her husband

Mr. Dabney and preferred her old woodburning cookstove to the new gas ranges. Every morning of my early life I woke to the sound of her beating batter-bread down in the kitchen.

Papa Dabney owned the largest shoe store in the South. In the children's department on the second floor he had a foot-powered merry-go-round that I loved to play on. Other days he would take me to the Acca railroad yards near our house to watch the switch engines on the old Richmond, Frederick and Potomac.

The other member of the household was Miss Williams, the practical nurse who had come home from the hospital with me, a sickly premature infant not expected to live. Papa Dabney liked to tell how I was so small they had carried me home in a Florsheim shoe box. Miss Williams had silver-rimmed spectacles and a lump in her nose where it had been broken and poorly set. She raised me on a bottle, in Richmond at that time an unheard-of innovation, afterwards stayed on to care for Mary Jane and me.

When I was seven years old, Dad remarried. Mary Jane and I went to live with him and our stepmother in a small house on Brook Road, and Miss Williams went to work for someone else. But I still spent nearly every weekend with Papa and Mama Dabney at Moss Side. And slowly, over the years, I watched Papa Dabney grow twisted and bent with a disease no one could cure.

They called it rheumatoid arthritis. When I was small it was only in his legs and he got around on crutches. Then it spread into his shoulders and hands and he had to live in a wheelchair. As I grew bigger I would lift him from the chair into his "cyah" or into his bed, and that's when I'd see how much it hurt. Not that Papa Dabney ever said anything; he was the most uncomplaining person on earth. In fact his doctor used to bring other patients to visit the badly crippled old man so that he cou'd cheer them up. But he would wince and his face would go hite, and that's when I made up my mind to become a doctor.

It was too late now to do anything for Papa Dabney. He had died three years ago when I was seventeen. I remembered coming home from a weekend scout trip to find my young half-brother Henry and my little half-sister Bruce Gordon at the front window. Henry was only seven and Bruce Gordon five and probably they were too young to realize exactly what had happened, but I saw at once that both of them had been crying. Dad, Mother, and Mary Jane, they told me, were over at Moss Side.

They had laid Papa Dabney out in the front parlor. I had stood in the doorway of the familiar room a long time, feeling a strange reluctance to step inside. The grey metal coffin stood on trestles next to the old Edison phonograph. At last I crossed to it and stood looking down at my grandfather.

But this pale, quiet figure was not Papa Dabney! He was too silent, too drained of color. His hands especially shocked me. The undertaker had straightened out the crippled fingers so that they lay flat on the shining satin. Papa Dabney's hands, twisted as they were, had been beautiful to me. These hands were too smooth, too waxy white, and to me they were terrifying.

But though I would never have a chance to help my grandfather, at least he had made me aware of the suffering in the world. And if, as I was finding out now, a man could make money in the act of preventing suffering, that was simply the wonderful justice of the way the universe was set up.

It was funny, in fact . . . as soon as I found out about the money side of it, I had begun thinking about all the things I'd like to own. I had a pretty good list now, starting with a Cadillac car, a swimming pool and a boat.

The ward boy was wheeling the noon meal into the large room and I put aside my dreams of high living long enough to concentrate on the tin plate in front of me. But when lunch was over the heady thoughts returned. On this accelerated Army program, I calculated, I'd be one of the youngest doctors ever to graduate. And then—well, the war couldn't last forever.

I looked down at the ring on my left hand: on an oval of black onyx was the golden owl of the Phi Gamma Delta fraternity, with the words "University of Richmond 1945" running around the base. Like many of the class of '45, here I was through school and in uniform by 1943! If I started med school this month and finished in three years . . . I figured by the time I was twenty-five I could have that Cadillac.

December 16. I took the stack of train schedules from the bedside table and went over them for the hundredth time. But no matter how I figured it, there was just no way to get from Abilene, Texas to Richmond, Virginia in under 30 hours. Actually with wartime travel, especially right around Christmas, I'd be lucky to do it in 48. That meant December 19 was positively the last day I could leave Abilene. And instead of a cold, doctors were now calling what I had, influenza.

Then, unexpectedly, on the morning of December 17th,

the silver thread of mercury in the slender glass tube stopped at 98.6°. The dayshift nurse reported the good news at once to the O.D., the medical officer on duty. In a few minutes he appeared at my bedside.

"I'm taking you personally over to Recuperation," he said.

He shouldered my duffel himself and set out through a maze of wooden corridors, me trotting after him with my boots and overcoat. I could hardly believe that these men and women, officers all of them, were going to so much trouble for a lowly private, but the doctor assured me that if my temperature stayed down he would speed up the discharge process and have me out of there the following day.

The recuperation ward I'd been moved to was identical to look at with the one I'd just left, twelve beds along each wall, twenty-four white-painted chairs, twenty-four bedside tables each with its table lamp and small night-light. The same three offices where you came in, with the three private cubicles across from them. Only here, because we were convalescents, we were free to come and go to other parts of the huge hospital complex—the hospital PX, for example, or the movie theatre, several connected buildings away. I spent the day sitting on the side of my bed, though. It was snowing outside and I wasn't taking a chance on catching cold again in some drafty corridor.

I kept thinking about Christmas, how great it would be to be back in Richmond. I was sure they would give the med students the day off on Christmas, and since Richmond was my hometown that meant I could be with my family.

Dad was away of course, but Mother would be there. She was actually my stepmother, and we hadn't always gotten along too well, but sitting in a wooden hospital barracks in Texas with sleet pinging against the windows, 1 realized that I missed her.

Mary Jane and her new husband might even get down from Fort Belvoir, Virginia. I really missed Mary Jane. I even missed Henry and Bruce Gordon. I had been jealous of them both ever since they were born; now that my stepmother had children of her own I was sure she didn't care as much about me. But on Christmas—well, it would be great to watch them come whooping down the stairs.

At lights-out a nurse came through the recuperation ward taking temperatures and writing them in a notebook. It was part of the routine—they had been doing it at intervals all day—and I thought nothing of it until a ward boy appeared at my bed with my duffel bag and other gear under his arm.

"We got to go to Isolation," he said.

I stared at him. "What do you mean?"

"You have a fever. I've got to take you to an isolation ward."

"But—my fever's gone! I'm checking out tomorrow!"

With a shrug he went to find the nurse. This time I read the thermometer myself: 103°.

I followed the soldier numbly down a lot of long wooden hallways and into a barracks identical to the other two I'd been in. I had hoped at least he was taking me back to the ward I'd left that morning, where the staff had taken such an interest in me, but although this one looked exactly the same, I realized after looking around a minute that it was not. There was so much influenza in camp right now, the ward boy said, that any bed was filled the minute it was vacated.

I got into the one he pointed out to me, but sleep was out of the question. Now what was I going to do? Tomorrow was the 18th. I'd never be on that original train—and what if I missed the one on the 19th too?

All night I tossed miserably, my own cough and the coughing of the men around me keeping me awake. Why would my fever suddenly shoot up again? From pre-med I knew that influenza could develop without warning into pneumonia, and that when that happened there wasn't an awful lot anyone could do. A few doctors were said to be experimenting with some new drugs, but they weren't yet in general use. If this turned into pneumonia—well, no telling how long I'd have to stay here.

But the next morning, December 18th, my fever was down some, not enough to move me back to Recuperation, but enough to keep my hopes up. I told the new nurses about the deadline in Richmond and they were as sympathetic as the others had been. By nighttime there was a concerned little group of staff people all taking time over my problem. Poring over the schedules, someone discovered a train leaving Abilene the night of the 19th—actually it would be early morning of the 20th—at 4:00 A.M. With a few lucky breaks it might get me to Richmond just in time.

"I could arrange to have a Jeep pick you up right here at the hospital," one of the doctors said. "If your temperature keeps going down we'll move you to Recuperation in the morning—that'll be the 19th—and you can go straight to the train station from there tomorrow night without reporting back to your company barracks at all."

And wonder of wonders, on the morning of the 19th my temperature once more registered normal! True to the doctor's word, I was moved immediately to a recuperation ward, gear and all, with a Jeep requisitioned to pick me up from there at 3:20 the following morning.

It was the fourth bed I'd been assigned to in this warren of a hospital and outwardly it was no different from the rest. Twelve beds in this row, twelve across the aisle. Three offices down there near the door, three little spaces opposite for serious cases. But to me this monotonous arrangement was the most beautiful room in the world. Here, this very night, a Jeep was coming to take me away from dust storms and drill fields forever.

That afternoon I put my uniform on, just to get used to wearing clothes again. I tried to make myself rest but I was too excited to sit still for long. About 5:00 the guy in the next bed suggested we kill some time by going to the movies. The first time I'd been in a recuperation ward I had scarcely dared move for fear I'd get sick again. This time I jumped at anything that would make the waiting go quicker. The suspense of these last few days, almost getting discharged, landing back in Isolation, now back to Recuperation, was really getting to me.

We went to the early show, right after supper, because I wanted to get to sleep early. I can't even remember what the picture was. I only know that as we sat there in the movie theatre I had this violent coughing attack.

We got back to the ward around 9:15, me with my fingers crossed that the nurse had finished her rounds for the night. Only the ward boy was on duty and I breathed a sigh of relief. I felt as though I might be running a fever again and I didn't want anyone sticking a thermometer in my mouth.

I went to the ward boy's little room and asked for some aspirin. He gave me six of them and three APC tablets (aspirin, phenacetin and caffeine), the only medication he was allowed to dispense. I got my duffel bag, too, from the back of his room, and my ankle-high GI boots and olive-drab overcoat, and piled them at the foot of my bed. Then I folded my uniform on the chair ready to put on in the middle of the night.

One of the nurses had loaned me an alarm clock and I double-checked to make sure it was set for 3:00 A.M. Finally I took two of the aspirin and one of the APC pills and, in spite of the fact that most of the guys in the ward were still up and walking around, got into bed and in a second was asleep.

III

A spasm of coughing woke me up. I groped for the sputum cup on the bedside table and spit something into it. My head ached and my chest felt like it was on fire. The ward was quiet and dark, only the small night-light burning beside each bed, twelve little halos of light along each wall.

What time was it? I peered at the alarm clock but it was too dark to see. I picked up the clock and held it closer to the night-light.

Midnight.

I poured a glass of water from the jug on the table, swallowed two more aspirin and another APC tablet and lay back down, noticing for the first time that my sheets were drenching wet. I kept having to sit up and spit into the cup. At last I must have dozed off because I woke up suddenly struggling for air. When the coughing attack passed I read the clock again. Ten after two.

Less than an hour till I had to get up. I was feeling lousy, sweat pouring off me and my heart going like a jackhammer. I took the last of the aspirin and tried to go back to sleep but I kept coughing up something from deep in my chest, and then I'd have to grab for the cup. At last I propped the pillow behind me and sat up. That seemed to help the coughing, but I ached all over and I knew for sure I was running a fever. Just so long as no one else found out till I was safely aboard that train!

I looked at the clock again. Almost time to start dressing. I punched off the alarm. No use disturbing everyone else so long as I was awake already. I stood up, wondering if I dared to switch on the table lamp to dress by. If this coughing hadn't waked people, I didn't suppose anything would. I turned on the light and walked around the bed to the chair, puzzled to find my legs trembling. I picked up my uniform and moved cautiously back to the bed table. I felt dizzy all over. I'd have to be careful or the Jeep driver would notice something. I stopped, staring down at the table.

The sputum cup was filled to the top with bright red blood.

A light was coming from the supply room near the door. I walked down there and looked in. The night ward boy was reading a magazine. "Lend me a thermometer for a sec?" I said.

He stood up and reached one down from a shelf. I walked a few feet away before putting it in my mouth: this was strictly for my own information. After a minute I read the temperature in the light from the supply room doorway.

Or tried to. I couldn't make sense of it. No matter how

I twisted the thermometer the silver shaft of mercury seemed to go right to the end. The ward boy came up behind me and took it out of my hand.

"A hundred and six and a half!" he yelped, and before I could stop him he was racing out the double doors into the corridor.

In a minute he was back with the night-duty nurse at his heels. She got another thermometer from the shelf in the supply room and looked at her watch while I held the little tube under my tongue cursing myself for a brainless fool. She pulled it out of my mouth and took one look at it.

"Sit down!" she said.

She steered me like a small child to the chair the ward boy had been using. "You stay with him," she told him. "I'll be right back!"

"I can't wait around here," I told the soldier as she disappeared. "I've got to get dressed! I've got a train to catch in exactly an hour."

"Just take it easy," he said. "The doctor's on his way."

What was the matter with the guy? Hadn't he heard me? "I'm going in to Abilene! A Jeep's picking me up in twenty minutes!"

"That's right," he said, "just sit still and everything will be OK."

The lunatic wouldn't pay any attention to me, and when the doctor arrived it was the same thing. He listened to my chest, then started talking about X-rays.

"He'll never walk that far," he said to the nurse. "We'd better get an ambulance here."

The nurse made a phone call while I tried to explain to them that it wasn't an ambulance I was waiting for, but a Jeep. I was still talking when two soldiers came running in with a stretcher. The doctor told me to lie down on it, which was really crazy when I ought to be getting into my uniform. But a private doesn't argue with a captain, so I lay down and they put some blankets around me and picked the thing up.

Next minute I felt cold night air on my face and they were sliding me into the back of an ambulance and we were bouncing along a road. A short while later the doors opened and again I felt that icy blast of air. They carried me through some doors and set the stretcher down in a room full of machinery. A man in a white coat leaned over me.

"Do you think you can stand up just for a minute?" he said.

I almost laughed as the two stretcher-bearers got their arms under mine and lifted me to my feet. I'd be standing a lot longer than a minute down at that train station in a little while!

Still holding my arms they walked me over to an upright metal panel with a shallow indentation on top for a chin rest. The man in white measured me with his eyes. "Six foot two," he said, turning a crank in the side of the contraption to raise it a bit. He tapped the little hollow on top.

"Can you get your chin over that? That's right. Now hold still just for a second."

The men let go my arms and stepped with the technician behind a partition. I heard a click and a whirr.

The whirr went on and on. It was getting louder. The whirr was inside my head and my knees were made of rubber. They were bending and I was falling and all the time the whirr grew louder.

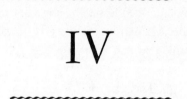

IV

I sat up with a start. What time was it? I looked at the bedside table but they'd taken the clock away. In fact . . . where was any of my stuff? The train schedules. My watch!

I looked around. I was in a tiny little room I'd never seen before. By the glow of the night-light I could see that this one bed practically filled it. There was a white wooden chair by the doorway, the bed, the table, and that was all.

Where was I?

And how had I gotten there?

I thought back trying to remember. The X-ray machine—that's right! They had taken me to the X-ray department and . . . and I must have fainted or something.

The train! I'd miss the train! I jumped out of bed in alarm, looking for my clothes. The X-ray people didn't know, of course, about the train; that's why they had put me in here instead of sending me back where the Jeep was waiting.

My uniform wasn't on the chair. I looked beneath it. Behind it. No duffel bag either. Where else in this little closet of a room could they have put them? Under the bed maybe? I turned around, then froze.

Someone was lying in that bed.

I took a step closer. He was quite a young man, with short brown hair, lying very still. But . . . the thing was impossible! I myself had just gotten out of that bed! For a moment I wrestled with the mystery of it. It was too strange to think about—and anyway I didn't have time.

The ward boy! Maybe my clothes were in his room! I hurried out of the little room and looked around. Two rows of night lights shone against the walls in the ward. I didn't think I'd ever been in this one before, but it was hard to tell, they all looked so much alike.

Directly across from me the supply room door was open, the light on, but no ward boy. I stepped inside, but the shelves held only the usual equipment, no clothing or shoes to be seen. The doctor's and nurse's offices were both dark —no one there either. I walked quietly down the aisle of sleeping soldiers in the large room, wondering if they could have put my stuff out here somewhere. But the light was too dim to see much. Except for some snores and an occasional cough there wasn't a sound.

I went back past the offices and stepped out into the corridor. A sergeant was coming along it carrying an instrument tray covered with a cloth. Probably he didn't know anything, but I was so glad to find someone awake that I started toward him.

"Excuse me, Sergeant," I said. "You haven't seen the ward boy for this unit, have you?"

He didn't answer. Didn't even glance at me. He just kept coming, straight at me, not slowing down.

"Look out!" I yelled, jumping out of his way.

The next minute he was past me, walking away down the corridor as if he had never seen me, though how we had kept from colliding I didn't know.

And then I saw something that gave me a new idea. Farther down the corridor was one of the heavy metal doors that led to the outside. I hurried toward it. Even if I had missed that train, I'd find some way of getting to Richmond!

Almost without knowing it I found myself outside, racing swiftly along, traveling faster in fact than I'd ever moved in my life. It wasn't as cold as it had been earlier in the evening—felt neither cold nor hot, actually.

Looking down I was astonished to see not the ground, but the tops of mesquite bushes beneath me. Already Camp Barkeley seemed to be far behind me as I sped over the dark frozen desert. My mind kept telling me that what I was doing was impossible, and yet . . . it was happening.

A town flashed by beneath me, caution lights blinking at the intersections. This was ridiculous! A human being couldn't fly without an airplane—anyhow I was traveling too low for a plane.

The countryside appeared more wooded now: broad snow-dusted fields surrounded by dark trees. Occasionally I'd see a road, but there was little traffic at this time of night, and the towns I passed were dark and silent.

I was going to Richmond; somehow I had known that

from the moment I burst through that hospital door. Going to Richmond a hundred times faster than any train on earth could take me.

But . . . now that I thought about it, how could I be sure that this was the way to Richmond? I had traveled between Texas and Virginia only once, going the other way, and a large part of that train trip had been at night. What made me think I could find my way back to Richmond all by myself?

An extremely broad river was below me now. There was a long, high bridge, and on the far bank the largest city I had come to yet. I wished I could go down there and find someone who could give me directions.

Almost immediately I noticed myself slowing down. Just below me now, where two streets came together, I caught a flickering blue glow. It came from a neon sign over the door of a red-roofed one-story building with a "Pabst Blue Ribbon Beer" sign propped in the front window. "Cafe," the jittering letters over the door read, and from the windows light streamed onto the pavement.

Staring down at it, I realized I had stopped moving altogether. Finding myself somehow suspended fifty feet in the air was an even stranger feeling than the whirlwind flight had been. But I had no time to puzzle over it, for down the sidewalk toward the all-night cafe a man came briskly walking. At least, I thought, I could find out from him what town this was and in what direction I was heading. Even as the idea occurred to me—as though thought and motion had become the same thing—I found myself down on the sidewalk, hurrying along at the stranger's side. He was a civilian, maybe forty or forty-five, wearing a topcoat but no hat. He was obviously thinking hard about something because he never glanced my way as I fell into step beside him.

"Can you tell me, please," I said, "what city this is?"

He kept right on walking.

"Please sir!" I said, speaking louder, "I'm a stranger here and I'd appreciate it if—"

We reached the cafe and he turned, reaching for the door handle. Was the fellow deaf? I put out my left hand to tap his shoulder.

There was nothing there.

I stood there in front of the door, gaping after him as he opened it and disappeared inside. It had been like touching . . . thin air. Like no one had been there at all. And yet I had distinctly seen him, even to the beginnings of a black stubble on his chin where he needed a shave.

I backed away from the mystery of the substance-less man and leaned up against the guy wire of a telephone pole to think things through. My body went through that guy wire as though it too had not been there.

There on the sidewalk of that unknown city, I did some incredulous thinking. The strangest, most difficult thinking I had ever done. The man in the cafe, this telephone pole . . . suppose they were perfectly normal. Suppose I was the one who was—changed, somehow. What if in some impossible, unimaginable way, I lost my . . . my hardness. My ability to grasp things, to make contact with the world. Even to be seen! The fellow just now. It was obvious he never saw or heard me.

Neither, now that I was facing facts, had that sergeant, back at the hospital. It was as though, for both of them, I hadn't existed.

And if those two hadn't seen me, the bewildering thoughts went on, what made me think the people at the Medical College of Virginia would be able to see me? What was the sense in this headlong dash to Richmond, if when I got there I couldn't make anyone aware of me?

Christmas too—what if I got home for Christmas and even my own family couldn't see me? A terrifying loneliness swept over me. Somehow, some way I had to get back that—that solidness that other people saw and responded to.

And suddenly I remembered the young man I had seen in the bed in that little hospital room. What if that had been . . . me? Or anyhow, the material, concrete part of myself that in some unexplainable way I'd gotten separated from. What if the form which I had left lying in a hospital room in Texas was my own?

And if it were, how could I get back to it again? Why had I ever rushed off so unthinkingly!

I was moving again, speeding away from the city. Below me was the broad river. I appeared to be going back, back in the direction I had come from, and it seemed to me I was flashing across space even faster than before. Hills, lakes, farms slipped away beneath me as I sped in an unswerving straight line over the dark nighttime land.

At last the trees thinned out and with a glow of recognition I saw below me the mesquite bushes and waterless gullies of west Texas. There were the barracks roofs of Camp Barkeley, long dark silhouettes against the snow-covered ground. I was lower now; I was slowing down. I was standing in front of the base hospital.

I hurried inside. There was the admissions department where I had reported ten days ago. It was evidently still the middle of the night, because the offices were closed and

41

locked. I started off along the left-hand corridor, but stopped when I saw that it led to what looked like a staff dining room. Where was the ward I had awakened in earlier tonight?

At last at the end of several hallways I came to a large room that looked familiar. There was a sleeping form in each of the beds that lined the walls, but the one that I was looking for—the one I was now convinced belonged to me —was in one of the small single rooms near the door, that I was sure of. I looked eagerly in all three of these, but the first two were empty and in the last one was a man in traction, both legs encased in plaster casts.

I returned to the corridor and looked up and down, undecided. Where was that little room? What wing of the huge hospital was it in, even?

I racked my brain trying to remember something—anything—that would help me locate it, but it was no use. I would have been unconscious when they brought me there from the X-ray room, and when I woke up I had been so obsessed with the idea of getting to Virginia that I had rushed off without even a backward glance. The fact was that somewhere in over two hundred barracks there was one tiny room which was infinitely important to me—and it could be in any one of them at all.

And so began one of the strangest searches that can ever have taken place: the search for myself. From one ward to another of that enormous complex I rushed, pausing in each small room, stooping over the occupant of the bed, hurrying on. There were hundreds and hundreds of these narrow single-bed cubicles, each so like every other one, and the wards all so alike, that soon I became confused about which ones I had been to, and whether I was simply retracing my steps over and over.

And slowly a far more alarming truth began to register. I had never seen myself.

Not really. Not the way I saw other people. From my chest down I had seen myself "in the round" of course, but from the shoulders up, I now realized, I had seen only a two-dimensional mirror-image staring at me from a piece of glass. And occasionally a snapshot, equally two-dimensional. That was all. The roundedness, the living, space-filling presence of myself, I did not know at all.

And that, I now discovered, is the way we recognize each other. Not by the shape of the nose or the color of the eyes, but by the whole three-dimensional impact of all the features at once.

I knew my height and weight of course. "Six feet two, one hundred and seventy-eight pounds," I kept repeating, as though memorizing the description of a stranger. But what help was that when the person was lying in bed? Here were row after row of soldiers who all must be around that size. They were all of them, like me, in their late teens or early twenties, all of them in hospital pajamas under brown Army blankets, every one of them with a G.I. haircut.

The only thing I had to go by was that the form I was looking for had to be in one of the three small single rooms at the front of each ward. But in those rooms I had already seen a dozen men who looked exactly the way I imagined myself—and I had barely begun to search this labyrinth of a place. How would I know when I found myself? Could I have passed myself already without knowing it?

On and on I wandered, pausing, studying faces, turning

away. The loneliness I had felt in the unfamiliar city was now a mounting panic. I was cut off from everyone in the world, from the solidness of the physical earth itself, and now . . . even from my own identity.

If the person in the bed was heavyset, or if he had blonde hair, or freckles, I hurried quickly on. But in the dim glow of the night-light it wasn't always easy to see even that much. It was hopeless. I leaned against a wall (I had grown used to the fact that walls and furniture didn't hold me up, but the position was a habit), and cudgeled my memory for some mark, some physical characteristic, that would identify me alone among all these sleeping twenty-year-old soldiers. Some mark on my face or hands? A wart, maybe, or a scar?

The Phi Gamma Delta ring.

Of course! The black onyx oval with the golden owl . . . Why hadn't I thought of it before! I would have to start all over now, have to go back to every room where the guy in the bed looked like I believed I looked. I started back the way I'd come.

That is . . . I guessed this was the way. It was all so confusing: identical wards opening off identical corridors. In and out of the small single rooms I sped, sparing only a glance if the left hand was outside the covers. More often than not, however, it was hidden beneath the sheets and then I could only wait for the sleeper to change position.

Once I sat for a long time beside a dark-haired young man whose mouth and chin in the faint light reminded me of my father's. He was moaning slightly, sleeping on his left side, his left arm under the pillow, and the more I stared at him the more I was sure that this was my own physical self. Again and again I grabbed at that pillow, trying to jerk it away. My fingers closed only on air. At last he heaved

44

himself up on one elbow, groping for the water pitcher on the night table. On his left hand was a gold wedding band.

From ward to ward I continued my search. A number of the soldiers I passed were awake, staring silently at the ceiling, or sitting on the side of the bed smoking a cigarette. And it was these waking people who made my aloneness so terrible. It is one thing to step unnoticed into a room where someone is sleeping, another altogether to have him look right at you and give no sign that you exist. In the hallways I persisted in jumping aside when a nurse or an orderly approached. I knew now that we would not collide—could not even touch each other—but somehow the thought of someone walking through the very space where I was standing was more than I could cope with.

At last in my roaming I came to the X-ray department. The white-coated technician I had met earlier was sitting at a desk reading some papers in a clipboard. Here was the last human being who had spoken to me.

"Look at me!" I shouted at him. "I'm standing right here!"

He uncapped his pen and jotted something on the paper. Was it only a few hours ago that I had been carried into this room on a stretcher? Surely that was weeks ago. Years ago. Or . . . was it only minutes? Something was strange about time, too, in this world where rules about space and speed and solid mass were all suspended. I had lost all sense of whether an experience was taking a split second, or whether it was lasting for hours.

I felt reluctant to leave the only person I had yet recognized. But eventually, after how long I couldn't tell, I wandered on. More corridors, more wards: twelve beds along the right wall, twelve along the left, three offices at the end near the door, three rooms across from them. Sleeping men, wide-awake men, bored men, frightened men. But never the ring with the owl.

In one little cubicle, a young man was crying. Homesick, maybe. A lot of us cried, when we thought no one was watching us, especially now around Christmastime. In the next cubicle—no one. Bed stripped of sheets. In the last one—

I drew back, startled. There was someone in the bed, all right, but the sheet had been pulled all the way up over the head, leaving only his arms outside the blankets. Strangely rigid and straight those arms looked, unnatural, hands turned palms downward. . . .

On the third finger of the left hand was a small gold owl on an oval of black onyx.

V

Slowly I crept forward, eyes riveted on that hand. There was something terrible about it. Even in the dim night-light I could see that it was too white, too smooth. Where had I seen a hand like that before? Then I remembered: Papa Dabney lying in the parlor at Moss Side.

I backed toward the doorway. The man in that bed was dead! I felt the same reluctance I had the previous time at being in a room with a dead person. But . . . if that was my ring, then—then it was me, the separated part of me, lying under that sheet. Did that mean that I was . . .

It was the first time in this entire experience that the word "death" occurred to me in connection with what was happening.

But I wasn't dead! How could I be dead and still be

awake? Thinking. Experiencing. Death was different. Death was . . . I didn't know. Blanking out. Nothingness. I was me, wide awake, only without a physical body to function in.

Frantically I clawed at the sheet, trying to draw it back, trying to uncover the figure on the bed. All my efforts did not even stir a breeze in the silent little room.

At last in despair I sank down on the bed. Or did so mentally: actually my disembodied being made no contact with it. There, right there, was my own shape and substance, yet as distant from me as though we inhabited separate planets. Was this what death was? This separation of one part of a person from the rest of him?

I wasn't sure when the light in the room began to change; suddenly I was aware that it was brighter, a lot brighter, than it had been. I whirled to look at the nightlight on the bedside table. Surely a single 15-watt bulb couldn't turn out that much light?

I stared in astonishment as the brightness increased, coming from nowhere, seeming to shine everywhere at once. All the light bulbs in the ward couldn't give off that much light. All the bulbs in the world couldn't! It was impossibly bright: it was like a million welders' lamps all blazing at once. And right in the middle of my amazement came a prosaic thought probably born of some biology lecture back at the university: "I'm glad I don't have physical eyes at this moment," I thought. "This light would destroy the retina in a tenth of a second."

No, I corrected myself, not the light.

He.

He would be too bright to look at. For now I saw that it was not light but a Man who had entered the room, or rather, a Man made out of light, though this seemed no more possible to my mind than the incredible intensity of the brightness that made up His form.

The instant I perceived Him, a command formed itself in my mind. "Stand up!" The words came from inside me, yet they had an authority my mere thoughts had never had. I got to my feet, and as I did came the stupendous certainty: "You are in the presence of *the* Son of God."

Again, the concept seemed to form itself inside me, but not as thought or speculation. It was a kind of knowing, immediate and complete. I knew other facts about Him too. One, that this was the most totally male Being I had ever met. If this was *the* Son of God, then His name was Jesus. But . . . this was not the Jesus of my Sunday School books. That Jesus was gentle, kind, understanding—and probably a little bit of a weakling. This Person was power itself, older than time and yet more modern than anyone I had ever met.

Above all, with that same mysterious inner certainty, I knew that this Man loved me. Far more even than power, what emanated from this Presence was unconditional love. An astonishing love. A love beyond my wildest imagining. This love knew every unlovable thing about me—the quarrels with my stepmother, my explosive temper, the sex thoughts I could never control, every mean, selfish thought and action since the day I was born—and accepted and loved me just the same.

When I say He knew everything about me, this was simply an observable fact. For into that room along with His radiant presence—simultaneously, though in telling about it I have to describe them one by one—had also entered every single episode of my entire life. Everything that had ever happened to me was simply there, in full view, contemporary and current, all seemingly taking place at that moment.

How this was possible I didn't know. I had never before experienced the kind of space we seemed to be in. The little one-bed room was still visible, but it no longer confined us. Instead, on all sides of us was what I could only think of as a kind of enormous mural—except that the figures on it were three dimensional, moving and speaking.

And many of these figures seemed to be me. Transfixed I stared at myself standing at the blackboard in a third-grade spelling class. Receiving my Eagle badge in front of my scout troop. Wheeling Papa Dabney onto the verandah at Moss Side. I saw myself a tiny two-and-a-half pound infant, panting for breath in an incubator. Simultaneously (there seemed to be no earlier, no later) I saw myself lifted by Caesarean section from the womb of the ill and dying young woman whom I had never laid eyes on before.

I saw myself a few months older, sitting on the lap of a kind-faced woman with silver-rimmed spectacles and a crooked nose. The three-year-old girl playing on the floor beside us must be Mary Jane, though of course I couldn't remember her at that age. But Miss Williams looked exactly as I recalled her. She appeared in many of the scenes; with a burst of long-forgotten yearning I saw how much I loved her.

Side by side with these scenes I saw Dad bringing a tall slender brunette to Moss Side: the woman he was going to marry. I saw Mary Jane and me moving with them into the house at 4306 Brook Road, saw myself standing fearfully at the dining room window, longing to go outside but afraid of the boy next door.

Along with cheerful scenes were miserable ones. I

50

watched myself getting beaten up by that boy, watched my humiliation as my sister hurried from the house to fight my battles for me. I saw myself crying as Dad said goodbye for a week, two weeks, a month, his job forever taking him away.

Much of the misery originated in me. I saw myself turning away when my stepmother bent over to kiss me goodnight, saw the very thought itself: "I'm not going to love this woman. My mother died. Miss Williams went away. If I love her she'll leave me too." I watched myself at age ten, standing at that same dining room window while Dad went to the hospital to bring home Mother and our new brother Henry, saw myself deciding before I ever saw him that I wasn't going to like this newcomer.

There were other scenes, hundreds, thousands, all illuminated by that searing Light, in an existence where time seemed to have ceased. It would have taken weeks of ordinary time even to glance at so many events, and yet I had no sense of minutes passing.

I watched us move, the year I was twelve, to a new house in the west end of Richmond. I saw the new bicycle Papa and Mama Dabney gave me, saw myself a thousand times biking across the railroad bridge to see them at Moss Side.

I saw the afternoon I came home to the west end house to find the sidewalk littered with splinters of balsam wood, all that remained of the giant model airplane I had glued together strip by painstaking strip. I watched my fury at three-year-old Henry who had committed this outrage harden, as time passed, into a sullen withdrawal from the entire family.

There were episodes from my high school years—dates, chemistry exams, running the fastest mile in our school. I saw my graduation day, saw myself entering the University of Richmond. And all the while I watched myself hold my stiff-necked aloofness from Mother, from my brother Henry, even from little Bruce Gordon. I saw Dad coming home in his major's uniform, saw myself going down to the post office to enlist for active service. I watched the mustering-in process at Camp Lee, watched myself and hundreds of other recruits boarding the train for Camp Barkeley. . . .

Every detail of twenty years of living was there to be looked at. The good, the bad, the high points, the run-of-the-mill. And with this all-inclusive view came a question. It was implicit in every scene and, like the scenes themselves, seemed to proceed from the living Light beside me.

What did you do with your life?

It was obviously not a question in the sense that He was seeking information, for what I had done with my life was in plain view. In any case this total recalling, detailed and perfect, came from Him, not me. I couldn't have remembered a tenth of what was there until He showed it to me.

What did you do with your life?

It seemed to be a question about values, not facts: what did you accomplish with the precious time you were allotted? And with this question shining through them, these ordinary events of a fairly typical boyhood seemed not merely unexciting but trivial. Hadn't I done anything lasting, anything important? Desperately I looked around me for something that would seem worthwhile in the light of this blazing Reality.

It wasn't that there were spectacular sins, just the sexual hang-ups and secretiveness of most teenagers. But if there were no horrendous depths, there were no heights either. Only an endless, shortsighted, clamorous concern for myself.

52

Hadn't I ever gone beyond my own immediate interests, done anything other people would recognize as valuable? At last I located it, the proudest moment of my life:

"I became an Eagle Scout!"

Again, words seemed to emanate from the Presence beside me:

That glorified you.

It was true. I could see myself standing in the center of the award circle, flushed with pride, the admiring eyes of my family and friends turned on me. Me, me, me—always in the center. Wasn't there any time in my life when I had let someone else stand there?

I saw myself walking forward at a church service at age eleven, asking Jesus to be Lord of my life. But I saw how quickly that first excitement turned into a dull routine of church-on-Sunday. Worse, I saw the smugness and self-esteem that went with it. I was better than the kids who didn't come to church. I was even better than lots who did: there was my perfect-attendance pin to prove it.

I started to point out my pre-med courses, how I was going to be a doctor and help people. But visible alongside the classroom scenes was that Cadillac car and that private airplane—thoughts as observable as actions in that all-pervading Light.

And all at once rage at the question itself built up in me. It wasn't fair! Of course I hadn't done anything with my life! I hadn't had time. How could you judge a person who hadn't started?

The answering thought, however, held no trace of judgement. *Death,* the word was infinitely loving, *can come at any age.*

Well, sure. I knew that babies and little kids died. Somehow I had just always assumed that a full life span was in some way owed me.

"What about the insurance money coming when I'm seventy?" The words were out, in this strange realm where communication took place by thought instead of speech, before I could call them back. A few months ago I had taken out the standard life insurance policy offered to servicemen; in some subconscious part of me had I believed this piece of paper guaranteed life itself? If I'd suspected before that there was mirth in the Presence beside me, now I was sure of it: the brightness seemed to vibrate and shimmer with a kind of holy laughter—not at me and my silliness, not a mocking laughter, but a mirth that seemed to say that in spite of all error and tragedy, joy was more lasting still.

And in the ecstasy of that laughter I realized that it was *I* who was judging the events around us so harshly. It was I who saw them as trivial, self-centered, unimportant. No such condemnation came from the Glory shining round me. He was not blaming or reproaching. He was simply . . . loving me. Filling the world with Himself and yet somehow attending to me personally. Waiting for my answer to the question that still hung in the dazzling air.

What have you done with your life to show Me?

Already I understood that in my first frantic efforts to come up with an impressive answer, I had missed the point altogether. He wasn't asking about accomplishments and awards.

The question, like everything else proceeding from Him, had to do with love. How much have you loved with your life? Have you loved others as I am loving you? Totally? Unconditionally?

54

Hearing the question like that, I saw how foolish it was even to try to find an answer in the scenes around us. Why, I hadn't known love like this was possible. Someone should have told me, I thought indignantly! A fine time to discover what life was all about—like coming to a final exam and discovering you were going to be tested on a subject you had never studied. If this was the point of everything, why hadn't someone told me?

But though these thoughts rose out of self-pity and self-excuse, the answering thought held no rebuke, only that hint of heavenly laughter behind the words:

I did tell you.

But how? Still wanting to justify myself: how could He have told me and I not heard?

I told you by the life I lived. I told you by the death I died. And, if you keep your eyes on Me, you will see more. . . .

With a start I noticed that we were moving. I hadn't been aware of leaving the hospital, but now it was nowhere in sight. The living events of my life which had crowded round us had vanished too: instead we seemed to be high above the earth, speeding together toward a distant pinprick of light.

It wasn't like the out-of-the-body travel I'd experienced earlier. Then, my own thoughts had obsessed me. Then I'd seemed almost to skim the surface of the earth. Now we were higher, moving faster; and with my eyes on Him, as He commanded, this mode of movement no longer seemed strange or alarming.

The distant pinprick resolved itself into a large city toward which we seemed to be descending. It was still nighttime but smoke poured from factory chimneys and many buildings had lights burning on every floor. There was an ocean or a large lake beyond the lights; it could have been Boston, Detroit, Toronto, certainly no place I had ever been, but obviously I thought as we came close enough to see the crowded streets, one where war industries were operating around the clock.

In fact the streets were impossibly crowded. Just below us two men bore down on the same section of sidewalk and an instant later had simply passed through each other. It was the same inside the humming factories and office buildings—where I could see as easily as I could see the streets—too many people at the machines and desks. In one room a grey-haired man was sitting in an armchair dictating a letter onto a rotating cylinder. Standing behind him, not an inch away, another man, maybe ten years older, kept snatching repeatedly at the speaking tube as though he would tear it from the seated man's hand.

"No!" he was saying, "if you order a hundred gross they'll charge more. Take a thousand gross at a time. Pierce would have given you a better deal. Why did you send Bill on that Treadwell job?" On and on he went, correcting, giving orders, while the man in the chair appeared neither to see nor hear him.

I noticed this phenomenon repeatedly, people unaware of others right beside them. I saw a group of assembly-line workers gathered around a coffee canteen. One of the women asked another for a cigarette, begged her in fact, as though she wanted it more than anything in the world. But the other one, chatting with her friends, ignored her. She took a pack of cigarettes from her coveralls, and without ever offering it to the woman who reached for it so eagerly, took one out and lit it. Fast as a striking snake the woman who had been refused snatched at the lighted cigarette in the other one's mouth. Again she grabbed at it. And again . . .

With a little chill of recognition I saw that she was unable to grip it.

I thought of that guy wire on the telephone pole. The sheet on the hospital bed. I remembered myself yelling at a man who never turned to look at me. And then I recalled the people here in this town trying in vain to attract attention, walking along a sidewalk without occupying space. Clearly these individuals were in the same substance-less predicament I myself was in.

Like me, in fact, they were dead.

But—it was so very different from the way I had always imagined death. I watched one woman of maybe fifty following a man of about the same age down the street. She seemed very much alive, agitated and tearful, except that the man to whom she was addressing her emphatic words was oblivious to her existence.

"You're not getting enough sleep. Marjorie makes too many demands on you. You know you've never been strong. Why aren't you wearing a scarf? You should never have married a woman who thinks only of herself." There was more, much more, and from some of it I gathered that she was his mother, in spite of the fact that they appeared so nearly the same age. How long had she been following him this way? Was this what death was like—to be permanently invisible to the living, yet permanently wrapped up in their affairs?

"Lay not up for yourselves treasures on earth! For where your treasure is, there will your heart be also!" I'd never been any good at memorizing Scripture, but those words of Jesus from the Sermon on the Mount sprang into my mind now like an electric shock. Perhaps these insubstantial people—the businessman, the woman begging cigarettes, this mother—although they could no longer contact the earth, still had their hearts there. Did I? With a kind of terror I thought of that Eagle Scout badge. Being a Phi Gam. Getting into med school. Was my heart, the focus of my being, fixed on things like these?

Keep your eyes on Me, Jesus had told me as we set out on this extraordinary journey. And when I did, whenever I looked at Him, the terror vanished, although the dreadful question remained. Without Him before me, in fact, I could not have endured the things He was showing me. As fast as thought we travelled from city to city, seemingly on the familiar earth, even the part of the earth—the United States and possibly Canada—that I'd always known, except for the thousands of non-physical beings that I now observed also inhabiting this "normal" space. In one house a younger man followed an older one from room to room. "I'm sorry, Pa!" he kept saying. "I didn't know what it would do to Mama! I didn't understand."

But though I could hear him clearly, it was obvious that the man he was speaking to could not. The old man was carrying a tray into a room where an elderly woman sat in bed. "I'm sorry, Pa," the young man said again. "I'm sorry, Mama." Endlessly, over and over, to ears that could not hear.

In bafflement I turned to the Brightness beside me. But though I felt His compassion flow like a torrent into the room before us, no understanding lighted my mind.

Several times we paused before similar scenes. A boy trailing a teenaged girl through the corridors of a school. "I'm sorry, Nancy!" A middle-aged woman begging a grey-haired man to forgive her.

"What are they so sorry for, Jesus?" I pleaded. "Why do they keep talking to people who can't hear them?"

Then from the Light beside me came the thought: *They are suicides, chained to every consequence of their act.*

The idea stunned me, yet I knew it came from Him, not me, for I saw no more scenes like these, as though the truth He was teaching had been learned.

Gradually I began to notice something else. All of the living people we were watching were surrounded by a faint luminous glow, almost like an electrical field over the surface of their bodies. This luminosity moved as they moved, like a second skin made out of pale, scarcely visible light.

At first I thought it must be reflected brightness from the Person at my side. But the buildings we entered gave off no reflection, neither did inanimate objects. And then I realized that the non-physical beings didn't either. My own un-solid body, I now saw, was without this glowing sheath.

At this point the Light drew me inside a dingy bar and grill near what looked like a large naval base. A crowd of people, many of them sailors, lined the bar three deep, while others jammed wooden booths along the wall. Though a few were drinking beer, most of them seemed to be belting whiskies as fast as the two perspiring bartenders could pour them.

Then I noticed a striking thing. A number of the men standing at the bar seemed unable to lift their drinks to their lips. Over and over I watched them clutch at their shot glasses, hands passing through the solid tumblers, through the heavy wooden counter top, through the very arms and bodies of the drinkers around them.

And these men, every one of them, lacked the aureole of light that surrounded the others.

Then, the cocoon of light must be a property of physical bodies only. The dead, we who had lost our solidness, had lost this "second skin" as well. And it was obvious that these living people, the light-surrounded ones, the ones actually drinking, talking, jostling each other, could neither see the desperately thirsty disembodied beings among them, nor feel their frantic pushing to get at those glasses. (Though it was also clear to me, watching, that the non-solid people could both see and hear each other. Furious quarrels were constantly breaking out among them over glasses that none could actually get to his lips.)

I thought I had seen heavy drinking at fraternity parties in Richmond, but the way civilians and servicemen at this bar were going at it beat everything. I watched one young sailor rise unsteadily from a stool, take two or three steps, and sag heavily to the floor. Two of his buddies stooped down and started dragging him away from the crush.

But that was not what I was looking at. I was staring in amazement as the bright cocoon around the unconscious sailor simply opened up. It parted at the very crown of his head and began peeling away from his head, his shoulders. Instantly, quicker than I'd ever seen anyone move, one of the insubstantial beings who had been standing near him at the bar was on top of him. He had been hovering like a thirsty shadow at the sailor's side, greedily following every swallow the young man made. Now he seemed to spring at him like a beast of prey.

In the next instant, to my utter mystification, the springing figure had vanished. It all happened even before the two men had dragged their unconscious load from under the feet of those at the bar. One minute I'd distinctly seen two individuals; by the time they propped the sailor against the wall, there was only one.

Twice more, as I stared, stupefied, the identical scene was repeated. A man passed out, a crack swiftly opened in the aureole round him, one of the non-solid people vanished as he hurled himself at that opening, almost as if he had scrambled inside the other man.

Was that covering of light some kind of shield, then? Was it a protection against . . . against disembodied beings like myself? Presumably these substance-less creatures had once had solid bodies, as I myself had had. Suppose that when they had been in these bodies they had developed a dependence on alcohol that went beyond the physical. That became mental. Spiritual, even. Then when they lost that body, except when they could briefly take possession of another one, they would be cut off for all eternity from the thing they could never stop craving.

An eternity like that—the thought sent a chill shuddering through me—surely that would be a form of hell. I had always thought of hell, when I thought of it at all, as a fiery place somewhere beneath the earth where evil men like Hitler would burn forever. But what if one level of hell existed right here on the surface—unseen and unsuspected by the living people occupying the same space. What if it meant remaining on earth but never again able to make contact with it. I thought of that mother whose son couldn't hear her. The woman who wanted that cigarette. I thought of myself, caring only about getting to Richmond, unable to make anyone see me or help me. To want most, to burn with most desire, where you were most powerless—that would be hell indeed.

Not "would be," I realized with a start. Was. This *was* hell: And I was as much a part of it as these other discarnate creatures. I had died. I had lost my physical body. I existed now in a realm that would not respond to me in any way. . . .

But if this was hell, if there was no hope, then why was He here beside me? Why did my heart leap for joy each time I turned to Him? For He was overwhelmingly the chief impression of the journey. All the sights and shocks assailing me were nothing compared to the main thing that was going on. Which was, quite simply, falling in love with the Person beside me. Whichever way I looked, He remained the real focus of my attention. Whatever else I saw, nothing compared with Him.

And that was another of the things baffling me. If I could see Him, why couldn't everyone else? He was too bright for living eyes to look at—that I had realized right away. But surely the living people we passed must somehow sense the love streaming out to them like heat from a mighty fire!

And these others, the ones like me who no longer had physical eyes that could be destroyed, how could they help but see the burning Love and Compassion in their midst? How could they miss Someone closer, more brilliant than the noonday sun?

Unless . . .

For the first time it occurred to me to wonder whether something infinitely more important than I ever believed could have happened that day when at age eleven I walked forward to the altar of a church. Was it possible that I, in some real way, had actually been "born again," as the preacher said—given new eyes, whether I understood any of it or not?

Or, could these others see Him now too, if their attention was not all caught up in the physical world they had lost? "Where your heart is . . ." As long as my heart had been set on getting to Richmond by a certain date, I hadn't been able to see Jesus either. Maybe whenever our center of attention was on anything else, we could block out even Him.

We were moving again. We had left the Navy base with its circumference of seedy streets and bars, and were now standing, in this dimension where travel seemed to take no time at all, on the edge of a wide, flat plain. So far in our journeying we had visited places where the living and the dead existed side by side: indeed where disembodied beings, completely unsuspected by the living, hovered right on top of the physical things and people where their desire was focused.

Now, however, although we were apparently still somewhere on the surface of the earth, I could see no living man or woman. The plain was crowded, even jammed with hordes of ghostly discarnate beings; nowhere was there a solid, light-surrounded person to be seen. All of these thousands of people were apparently no more substantial than I myself. And they were the most frustrated, the angriest, the most completely miserable beings I had ever laid eyes on.

"Lord Jesus!" I cried. "Where are we?"

At first I thought we were looking at some great battlefield: everywhere people were locked in what looked like fights to the death, writhing, punching, gouging. It couldn't be a present day war because there were no tanks or guns. No weapons of any sort, I saw as I looked closer, only bare hands and feet and teeth. And then I noticed that no one was apparently being injured. There was no blood, no bodies strewed the ground; a blow that ought to have eliminated an opponent would leave him exactly as before.

Although they appeared to be literally on top of each other, it was as though each man was boxing the air; at last I realized that of course, having no substance, they could not actually touch one another. They could not kill, though they clearly wanted to, because their intended victims were already dead, and so they hurled themselves at each other in a frenzy of impotent rage.

If I suspected before that I was seeing hell, now I was sure of it. Up to this moment the misery I had watched consisted in being chained to a physical world of which we were no longer part. Now I saw that there were other kinds of chains. Here were no solid objects or people to enthrall the soul. These creatures seemed locked into habits of mind and emotion, into hatred, lust, destructive thought-patterns.

Even more hideous than the bites and kicks they exchanged, were the sexual abuses many were performing in feverish pantomime. Perversions I had never dreamed of were being vainly attempted all around us. It was impossible to tell if the howls of frustration which reached us were actual sounds or only the transference of despairing thoughts. Indeed in this disembodied world it didn't seem to matter. Whatever anyone thought, however fleetingly or unwillingly, was instantly apparent to all around him, more completely than words could have expressed it, faster than sound waves could have carried it.

And the thoughts most frequently communicated had to do with the superior knowledge, or abilities, or background of the thinker. "I told you so!" "I always knew!" "Didn't I warn you!" were shrieked into the echoing air over and over. With a feeling of sick familiarity I recognized here my own thinking. This was me, my very tone of voice—the righteous one, the award-winner, the churchgoer. At age twenty I hadn't yet developed any truly chaining physical habits, not like the beings I'd seen scrabbling to get close to that bar. But in these yelps of envy and wounded self-importance I heard myself all too well.

Once again, however, no condemnation came from the Presence at my side, only a compassion for these unhappy creatures that was breaking His heart. Clearly it was not His will that any one of them should be in this place.

Then—what was keeping them here? Why didn't each one just get up and leave? I could see no reason why the person being screamed at by that man with the contorted face didn't simply walk away. Or why that young woman didn't put a thousand miles between herself and the other one who was so furiously beating her with insubstantial fists? They couldn't actually hold onto their victims, any of these insanely angry beings. There were no fences. Nothing apparently prevented them from simply going off alone.

Unless . . . unless there was no "alone" in this realm of disembodied spirits. No private corners in a universe where there were no walls. No place that was not inhabited by other beings to whom one was totally exposed at all times. What was it going to be like, I thought with sudden panic, to live forever where my most private thoughts were not private at all? No disguising them, no covering them up, no way to pretend I was anything but what I actually was. How unbearable. Unless of course everyone around me had the same kind of thoughts. . . . Unless there was a kind of consolation in finding others as loathsome as one's self, even if all we could do was hurl our venom at each other.

Perhaps this was the explanation for this hideous plain. Perhaps in the course of eons or of seconds, each creature here had sought out the company of others as pride-and-hate-filled as himself, until together they formed this society of the damned.

Perhaps it was not Jesus who had abandoned them, but they who had fled from the Light that showed up their darkness. Or . . . were they as alone as at first it appeared? Gradually I was becoming aware that there was something else on that plain of grappling forms. Almost from the beginning I had sensed it, but for a long time I could not locate it. When I did it was with a shock that left me stunned.

That entire unhappy plain was hovered over by beings seemingly made of light. It was their very size and blinding brightness that had prevented me at first from seeing them. Now that I had, now that I adjusted my eyes to take them in, I could see that these immense presences were bending over the little creatures on the plain. Perhaps even conversing with them.

Were these bright beings angels? Was the Light beside me also an angel? But the thought which had pressed itself so undeniably on my mind in that little hospital room had been: "You are in the presence of *the* Son of God." Could it be that each of these other human wraiths, wretched and unworthy like me, was also in His presence? In a realm where space and time no longer followed any rules I knew, could He be standing with each of them as He was with me?

I didn't know. All I clearly saw was that not one of these bickering beings on the plain had been abandoned. They were being attended, watched over, ministered to. And the equally observable fact was that not one of them knew it.

If Jesus or His angels were speaking to them, they certainly did not hear. There was no pause in the stream of rancor coming from their own hearts; their eyes sought only some nearby figure to humiliate. It would have seemed to me impossible not to be aware of what were the hugest and most striking features of that whole landscape, except that I myself had stared at them unseeing.

In fact, now that I had become aware of these bright presences, I realized with bewilderment that I'd been seeing them all along, without ever consciously registering the fact, as though Jesus could show me at any moment only so much as I was ready to see. Angels had crowded the living cities and towns we had visited. They had been present in the streets, the factories, the homes, even in that raucous bar, where nobody had been any more conscious of their existence than I myself had.

And suddenly I realized that there was a common denominator to all these scenes so far. It was the failure to see Jesus. Whether it was a physical appetite, an earthly concern, an absorption with self—whatever got in the way of His Light created the separation into which we stepped at death.

VI

We were moving again. Or rather, the scene in front of us was—changing somehow. Opening up. It was the quality of light that was different, as though the air had suddenly become more transparent, enabling me to see what had apparently been there all along.

Again, it was as if Jesus could reveal only as much as my mind could grasp. First He had shown me a hellish realm, filled with beings trapped in some form of self-attention. Now behind, beyond, through all this I began to perceive a whole new realm! Enormous buildings stood in a beautiful sunny park and there was a relationship between the various structures, a pattern to the way they were arranged, that reminded me somewhat of a well-planned university.

Except that to compare what I was now seeing with anything on earth was ridiculous. It was more as if all the schools and colleges in the world were only piecemeal reproductions of this reality.

We seemed suddenly to have entered an altogether different dimension, almost another kind of existence. After the clamor of the wartime cities and the shrieking voices of the plain, here was an all-pervading peace. As we entered one of the buildings and started down a high-ceilinged corridor lined with tall doorways, the air was so hushed that I was actually startled to see people in the passageway.

I could not tell if they were men or women, old or young, for all were covered from head to foot in loose-flowing hooded cloaks which made me think vaguely of monks. But the atmosphere of the place was not at all as I imagined a monastery. It was more like some tremendous study center, humming with the excitement of great discovery. Everyone we passed in the wide halls and on the curving staircases seemed caught up in some all-engrossing activity; not many words were exchanged among them. And yet I sensed no unfriendliness between these beings, rather an aloofness of total concentration.

Whatever else these people might be, they appeared utterly and supremely self-forgetful—absorbed in some vast purpose beyond themselves. Through open doors I glimpsed enormous rooms filled with complex equipment. In several of the rooms hooded figures bent over intricate charts and diagrams, or sat at the controls of elaborate consoles flickering with lights. I'd prided myself a little on the beginnings of a scientific education; at the university I had majored in chemistry, minored in biology, studied physics and calculus. But if these were scientific activities of some kind, they were so far beyond anything I knew, that I couldn't even guess what field they were in. Somehow I felt that some vast experiment was being pursued, perhaps dozens and dozens of such experiments.

"What are they doing, Jesus?" I asked.

But although Knowing flamed from Him like fire—though in fact I sensed that every activity on this mighty "campus" had its source in God—no explanation lighted my mind. What was communicated, as before, was love: compassion for my ignorance, understanding that encompassed all my non-understanding.

And something more . . . In spite of His obvious delight in the beings around us, I sensed that even this was not the ultimate, that He had far greater things to show me if only I could see.

And so I followed Him into other buildings of this domain of thought. We entered a studio where music of a complexity I couldn't begin to follow was being composed and performed. There were complicated rhythms, tones not on any scale I knew. "Why," I found myself thinking, "Bach is only the beginning!"

Next we walked through a library the size of the whole University of Richmond. I gazed into rooms lined floor to ceiling with documents on parchment, clay, leather, metal, paper. "Here," the thought occurred to me, "are assembled the important books of the universe."

Immediately I knew this was impossible. How could books be written somewhere beyond the earth! But the thought persisted, although my mind rejected it. "The key works of the universe," the phrase kept recurring as we roamed the domed reading rooms crowded with silent scholars. Then abruptly, at the door to one of the smaller rooms, almost an annex: "Here is the central thought of this earth."

Out we moved again into the hushed and expectant park. Then into a building crowded with technological machinery. Into a strange sphere-shaped structure where a catwalk led us over a tank of what appeared to be ordinary water. Into what looked like huge laboratories and into what might have been some kind of space observatory. And as we went my sense of mystification grew.

"Is this . . . heaven, Lord Jesus?" I ventured. The calm, the brightness, they were surely heaven-like! So was the absence of self, of clamoring ego. "When these people were on earth did they grow beyond selfish desires?"

They grew, and they have kept on growing. The answer shone like sunlight in that intent and eager atmosphere. But if growth could continue, then this was not all. Then . . . there must be something even these serene beings lacked. And suddenly I wondered if it was the same thing missing in the "lower realm." Were these selfless, seeking creatures also failing in some degree to see Jesus? Or perhaps, to see Him for Himself? Bits and hints of Him they surely had; obviously it was the truth they were so single-mindedly pursuing. But what if even a thirst for truth could distract from the Truth Himself, standing here in their midst while they searched for Him in books and test tubes. . . .

I didn't know. And next to His unutterable love, my own bewilderment, all the questions I wanted to ask, seemed incidental. Perhaps, I concluded at last, He cannot tell me more than I can see: perhaps there is nothing in me yet that could understand an explanation.

The central fact, the all-adequate one, remained this Per-

sonality at my side. Whatever additional facts He was showing me, He remained every moment the real focus of my
attention.

Which is why, perhaps, I was not aware of the precise
moment when we left the surface of the earth. . . .

Up until this point I had had the impression that we were
traveling—though in what manner I could not imagine—
upon the earth itself. Even what I had come to think of as
a "higher plane" of deep thoughts and learning, was obviously not far distant from the "physical plane" where body-
less beings were still bound to a solid world.

Now however, we seemed to have left the earth behind.
I could no longer see it. Instead we appeared to be in an
immense void, except that I had always thought of that as
a frightening word, and this was not. Some unnameable
promise seemed to vibrate through that vast emptiness.

And then I saw, infinitely far off, far too distant to be
visible with any kind of sight I knew of . . . a city. A
glowing, seemingly endless city, bright enough to be seen
over all the unimaginable distance between. The brightness
seemed to shine from the very walls and streets of this
place, and from beings which I could now discern moving
about within it. In fact, the city and everything in it seemed
to be made of light, even as the Figure at my side was made
of light.

At this time I had not yet read the Book of Revelation.
I could only gape in awe at this faraway spectacle, wondering how bright each building, each inhabitant, must be to
be seen over so many light-years of distance. Could these
radiant beings, I wondered, amazed, be those who had indeed kept Jesus the focus of their lives? Was I seeing at last
ones who had looked for Him in everything? Looked so

well and so closely that they had been changed into His very likeness? . . . Even as I asked the question, two of the bright figures seemed to detach themselves from the city and start toward us, hurling themselves across that infinity with the speed of light.

But as fast as they came toward us, we drew away still faster. The distance increased, the vision faded. Even as I cried out with loss, I knew that my imperfect sight could not now sustain more than an instant's glimpse of this real, this ultimate heaven. He had shown me all He could; now we were speeding far away.

Walls closed around us. Walls so narrow and box-like, that it was several seconds before I recognized the little hospital room we had left what seemed a lifetime ago.

Jesus still stood beside me, otherwise consciousness could not have sustained the transition from infinite space to the dimensions of this cell-like room. The glorious city still sparkled and glowed in my thoughts, beckoning, calling. With total indifference I noticed that there was a figure lying beneath the sheet on the bed which nearly filled the minuscule room.

But incredibly Jesus was telling me that I belonged somehow with that sheeted form, that His purpose for me involved that lump-like thing as well. I was moving nearer to it. It was filling my field of vision, shutting off the Light. Desperately I cried out to Him not to leave me, to make me ready for that shining city, not to abandon me in this dark and narrow place.

As in a long-ago half-forgotten story I remembered myself combing the halls and wards of this very hospital, wanting desperately to find the figure on this bed. From that loneliest moment of my existence I had leapt into the most perfect belonging I had ever known. The Light of Jesus had entered my life and filled it completely, and the idea of being separated from Him was more than I could bear.

Even as I pleaded I felt consciousness slipping from me. My mind began to blur. . . . I no longer knew what I was struggling for. My throat was on fire and the weight on my chest was crushing me.

I opened my eyes but there was something in front of my face. I groped about the blankets trying to find what was covering me, but moving my arms was like trying to lift lead bars. At last my fingers closed upon each other. With my right hand I touched a circular band with an oval stone on the ring finger of my left hand. Slowly I twisted it round and round, as blackness closed over me.

VII

It had taken four sessions to relate this much of my story to Fred Owen. Throughout, he had stopped me to ask questions or offer interpretations—and to let me know he wasn't necessarily buying a word of it.

Now, however, he sat absolutely still, while on my desk the numbers on the digital clock flipped over. I heard the outer door open and close as my next patient arrived. I looked at the clock: we had ten more minutes.

"You had . . . returned to your body?" Fred asked at last.

"That's the way I interpret it now," I said. "At the time I didn't know much of anything. For the next two or three days I was pretty much unconscious. Just some feverish, nightmarish kinds of dreams—the kind of thing you'd expect with a serious illness."

That was the main thing, I told him. When I began to be conscious again I was mostly conscious of being *sick.* My physical problems crowded everything else out of my head. But while I'd been—out of the body? I didn't know how else to describe it—there was no pain. No physical feeling of any kind.

The next thing I could recall for sure, I went on, was opening my eyes with a mammoth headache and seeing a nurse smiling down at me.

"It's good to have you back with us," she said. "For a while there we didn't think you were going to make it."

I licked my fever-cracked lips. "What day is this?" I rasped out.

"This is Christmas Eve, Private Ritchie." Holiday leave for the hospital staff had been cancelled, she added, because of the influenza epidemic and a heavy incidence of pneumonia in the camp.

I tried to think of another question so she wouldn't leave. Somehow I had to communicate to her the thing that had happened to me. Yes, she said, they'd had snow almost every day. Her name, she told me, was Lieutenant Irvine.

"I've just had the most astounding experience," I plunged in. "Something everyone on earth has to know about."

A coughing attack seized me. Lieutenant Irvine had to get her arm under my back and prop me up to give me a drink of water. "Don't talk any more now," she said. "I'll look in on you later."

And actually, I wondered, what was I going to say? "I've just seen God? I've been to hell? I've had a glimpse of heaven?" She'd think I was crazy.

All that week, whenever anyone came into that little room, I tried to describe the Light that had filled this very space, and the all-essential question He had asked. I never got beyond the first few words.

"Get some rest now. Don't try to talk," the doctor or nurse would say—and indeed my voice was no more than a gasping croak. The staff was obviously more interested in matters like my metabolic rate, my temperature, the amount of intravenous fluid I was getting. It was evident from the attention I was getting that this was considered more than a routine case. And gradually, as the days passed, I pieced together what had happened on the hospital floor during the time when I, on my side of the event, was meeting Jesus.

"Our time's up for today," I told Fred, "but tomorrow if you like I'll tell you what I found out from the doctors."

Fred was coming daily now, though even the short walk from the parking lot left him breathless. So it was the following afternoon that I resumed my story. . . .

VIII

After I collapsed in front of the X-ray machine, I learned I had been taken to a small isolation room in a nearby ward where my condition was diagnosed as double lobar pneumonia. Over the next twenty-four hours, in spite of all the hospital could do—in 1943 "miracle drugs" were still in their infancy—my condition deteriorated.

Early in the morning of December 21, twenty-four hours after I had been carried unconscious to the little room, the ward boy making his regular rounds to hand out medication, arrived at my little cubicle and failed to find a pulse. He checked my respiration rate. None. Next he took my blood pressure. Again, none, at which point he went running for the officer on duty.

The O.D. arrived on the double and re-ran the tests

himself with the same results. At last he straightened up. "He's dead, all right," he told the ward boy. "When you finish your rounds get him ready for the morgue."

He spoke heavily: already there had been a number of deaths at Camp Barkeley that month. Reluctantly he straightened my arms along the blankets, pulled the sheet up to cover my face, and returned to the ward to do what he could for the living.

The ward boy too continued on his rounds. And that must have been the point at which I, in my desperate disembodied search, arrived back at that little room and saw a figure covered with a sheet. . . .

Approximately nine minutes later, according to the hospital records, the ward boy returned to the little room to begin prepping the body for transfer to the morgue. But— surely that hand on the blanket has moved?

Again the ward boy went galloping for the O.D. The officer returned with him, examined me a second time, for the second time pronounced me dead. Doubtless the young orderly on the long, lonely night shift, was imagining things.

And then occurred the event the full impact of which only registered with me years later. At the time I learned of it I was surprised certainly, but not dumfounded as I am today each time I think of it.

The ward boy refused to accept the verdict of his superior officer. "Maybe," he suggested, "you could give him a shot of adrenalin directly into the heart muscle."

It was unthinkable, in the first place, for a private to argue with an officer, especially on a medical matter when the private was an untrained ward boy and the officer a licensed physician. In the second place what the ward boy was suggesting was medically ridiculous. In those days before widespread use of cardiac massage and electric shock, adrenalin injected into the heart was, it is true, occasionally attempted in cases of heart arrest. But this was only done when the heart had stopped because of some trauma to a basically healthy patient, like a drowning accident, where getting the heart started again holds out some hope for ultimate recovery.

But when the entire system has deteriorated from an illness like pneumonia, simply getting the heart muscle to contract a few more times achieves nothing. Technically you may get a heart beat for a few minutes, but you have not altered the overall condition. Indeed my condition, any medical man would have known, was totally irreversible; after so long without oxygen the brain would be hopelessly damaged.

And yet this knowledgeable O.D., fully aware of the unreasonableness of what he was doing, accepted the suggestion of the uninformed enlisted man at his side. "Get a sterile pack from the supply room!" he told him. When the ward boy reappeared, the officer filled the hypodermic from a vial of adrenalin, then plunged the hollow needle into my heart.

Erratically at first, beating resumed. Then as the two watched, incredulous, it settled into a rhythmic pulse.

A moment later respiration commenced. My blood pressure rose. My breathing grew stronger. . . .

It was by no means an instant recovery. It was three days before I was conscious, five before I was off the critical list, two weeks before I was walking. But only now, with twenty-seven years of my own medical practice behind me, can I appreciate the bewilderment with which the staff must have followed my progress. By the time I was well enough to ask questions, both the officer on duty that night, and the ward boy whose unaccountable hunch proved correct, had shipped with a unit bound overseas. But I received a personal visit from Dr. Donald G. Francy, the commanding officer to whom the O.D. had reported the events of the evening. Dr. Francy called my recovery "the most amazing medical case I ever encountered," and in a notarized statement years later wrote, "Private George G. Ritchie's . . . virtual call from death and return to vigorous health has to be explained in terms of other than natural means."

IX

At the time, however, I told Fred Owen, the details of my recovery interested me very little. I regarded my return to this life as a calamity; would have been angry, if I'd had the strength, with those who labored to revive me.

Mostly I just lay in bed, a very sick young man, wrestling with the immense Encounter I had had in that very cubicle. Thinking of Jesus. Wishing I knew how to tell others about Him. Wondering how I could live where I could not see Him.

The times when my separation from Him seemed easiest to bear, was when somebody came into the room. Ward boys, nurses, doctors, it didn't matter, my heart gave a leap whenever someone appeared. Lieutenant Irvine—Retta was her first name, I found out, though of course I never dared use it—was especially faithful about "looking in" as she put it, and each time I tried again to tell her what had happened to me. "It was like the brightest sun you've ever seen, only not a burning sun. . . ." The trouble was I lacked words to express even the faintest part of it, and I could see that my attempts only puzzled her.

Thinking back I realize Retta Irvine can't have been more than twenty-six or twenty-seven, a pretty blonde with a trim figure and a delectable smile, but to my young eyes she seemed practically middle-aged, an older woman to whom I could pour out my troubles. Since I couldn't make her understand about the Light and the worlds He had shown me, I told her about med school and how I was to have started classes three weeks before. That she sympathized with at once. It was great, talking to her. To look in a human face and have her look at me, to speak and see her react, why hadn't I realized the wonder of it before?

As soon as I was able to totter unsteadily out to the main ward, my spirits improved still more, and I began to pester them into moving me to one of the regular beds where I would have people on both sides of me. I was amazed, remembering myself as I had been up to this experience: a shy, rather introverted person. Only in scouting and in the Phi Gams had I been at ease with other people, and that was because I had been with the same group day after day. Now suddenly I found myself greeting total strangers like lifelong buddies. The utter aloneness I had known as I roamed these same wards unseen, unthought of, had made a deep turnabout change in me.

When lights went out each night and conversation died away, I would lie staring at the row of night-lights across the aisle, thinking back over every detail of that extraordinary night when Light itself had entered this drab wooden barracks. Was He still here? I wondered. Was it only because He was too dazzling for physical eyes that none of us could see Him?

I had grown discouraged about even attempting to tell others what I had seen. Discouraged and a little self-protective too. I was enjoying the new-found companionship of the ward too much to risk being ostracized as an oddball. But for hours each night I'd recall every sight, every sound of that incredibly vivid time. First that hellish realm, where I'd been permitted to look longest. Where people who no longer belonged to the earth could not escape it either—couldn't escape the involvements, the hungers, the pride they had allowed to dominate them here. Then the brief visit to a realm where ego had been left behind, where all was selfless search for truth. Where I might almost have thought myself in heaven except for that final fleeting revelation. The glorious city. I had seen it for an instant only, yet of the whole experience it stood out clearest. Most achingly.

What did it all mean? Why should such things have been shown to me, of all people? Above all, what was I supposed to do about it now?

That was the question Fred Owen was asking, slumped in the armchair next to mine, timing his words between labored breaths.

"Did it make any real difference? In your life, I mean. In what you did. Otherwise it's all very fascinating, having an inside track to God and all that, but I can't see that it matters very much."

An inside track. . . . Did I detect a note of—envy—in

those words? If so, it was obvious I had failed to get across the essence of the experience.

This was no round trip to heaven, I reminded Fred. If I saw heaven at all, it was only at an enormous distance, unattainable by the person I then was, or could conceive of becoming. Nor did I believe that as a boy of twenty I had peered into the depths of hell; I had not seen, for instance, the lake of fire recorded in the Bible.

But what I saw of the next life as it was apparently being experienced by people very like myself was hell enough. Enough to fill me with a lifelong terror of any attitude, habit, priority that would shape me for an existence like some of those I had seen. There had been no casual events for me since that night in Texas, I told Fred, no "unimportant" encounters with people. Every minute of every day since that time, I'd been aware of the presence of a larger world.

And strangely enough, it was the glory of that world, not the terror, which made my return to this life so hard. The contrast between the love of Jesus and the world in which I found myself having to go on living made the year following my illness the most difficult of my life. "What difference has it made?" Fred was asking me. To play it straight with him, as I had agreed to do, I knew I would have to tell Fred, and tell him honestly, about what happened next.

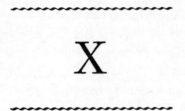

X

It was three weeks after my out-of-the-body encounter with Christ, that Lieutenant Irvine stopped at my bed with unhoped-for good news. The Medical College of Virginia had held my entrance position open for me! As soon as I could make the trip east I was to report for classes!

Once again my convalescence became a race against time: every day of missed classes meant more to make up, less chance of staying in the program. "You've got to eat," Lieutenant Irvine would say each time she saw me. "We're not allowed to show patients their charts, but I'll tell you for certain they won't let you out of here until you put on another fifteen pounds."

And so I ate, stuffing myself with mashed potatoes that stuck to my dry mouth like library paste, drinking milk until the sight of the metal urn made my stomach rise in my throat.

At last, one clear windy day in late January, exactly a month after I had been scheduled to start medical school, I received my official discharge from Camp Barkeley Hospital. I stood staring at the train ticket in my hands. The Army had reserved not just a seat but a sleeping berth for me leaving Abilene the following afternoon, an unheard-of luxury for a private and an indication of the fact that I had a lot of recovering still to do. My discharge weight was on my papers: 134 pounds. Forty-four less than the 178 I had checked in with. And 134, I knew, was at least 15 pounds higher than it had been. . . .

But the point was, I was going to med school: they had saved my place for me! I telephoned my stepmother to tell her what time the train got to Richmond. She had been writing regularly all the time I was in the hospital, saying she understood I was too ill to feel like answering. I was glad to let it go at that, glad for the hospital office which had kept her informed. I had never been much good at communicating with her.

I stared out the window of the Pullman as the countryside rolled past. Texarkana . . . Little Rock . . . Memphis . . . different trains, different engines picking up my coach as it travelled east.

In West Virginia we began to climb toward Charleston. And then we were over the state line into Virginia. Covington, Clifton Forge, Waynesboro—how beautiful it all was! The swollen streams, the forests where I had camped with my Scout troop. Then down the eastern slopes of the Blue Ridge to Charlottesville, and on at last to Richmond.

It was growing dark again when we reached the city, 48 hours after I had boarded the train in Abilene. Below the elevated track, rush hour traffic crawled bumper to bumper through the slushy streets. Ahead in the early winter twilight I made out the vast red brick bulk of the Main Street Depot. Heart hammering, I struggled into my overcoat. Whether from weakness or the excitement of being home, my legs were trembling and the weight of the coat nearly dragged me to the floor. Through the train window I could see that the station platform was jammed with travelers, most of them, like me, in uniform.

Then I saw my stepmother. Tall, thinner than I remembered her, her waist-length brown hair caught into a bun beneath her hat, she was trotting along the platform dragging ten-year-old Henry behind her.

I dragged my gear from beneath the seat and struggled down the train aisle; in Abilene they had assigned someone to carry the heavy duffel aboard for me. Mother spotted me as I came down the steps. Next moment her arms were around me, while Henry tried to climb up my back. Mother said nothing about my appearance but after a few steps she silently reached over and took the duffel bag from me. She led us to the elevator too, instead of taking the stairs down to the street, all the while filling me in on family news. Bruce Gordon was in bed with a cold. Christmas had been lonely with Dad and me away. Mama Dabney had invited me to Moss Side for breakfast next morning—"Batter bread you can be sure!"—before I had to report to med school at 9:00.

Later that night, when Henry and Bruce Gordon were

asleep, Mother and I sat in the living room with the Christmas eggnog she had saved till now.

"George?"

I looked up to find her brown eyes on mine. "Something's happened to you, George. Is it anything you can talk about?"

I gave a helpless little shrug. As a child I had always suspected she could read my mind. And all at once, there in that familiar room, with the photo of Dad on the mantel, a curious thing happened. After trying for weeks to describe to someone else my out-of-the-body experience, I suddenly found myself doing it. Telling my stepmother, this woman with whom I had resisted communicating all my life. Expressing to her what I hadn't been able to say to anyone else.

I heard myself describe how I had jumped out of bed and turned around to find a young man still lying there. I heard myself tell about the frantic flight toward Richmond. About returning to Camp Barkeley and searching for myself. About the Light, and the journey on which we set out . . .

She listened without a word to the entire account, scarcely shifting her position on the couch, searching my face with those eyes that missed nothing. And as I talked I was aware of something just as amazing as this torrent of words from a young man as tongue-tied as I was. It wasn't that she believed me, though she clearly did. It was something taking place in me, a startling change in viewpoint, so that all at once I was looking not at George Ritchie's stepmother, but at Mary Skeen Ritchie, a person with a life history of her own.

For the first time in my life I was seeing the courageous

young woman who had taken on not only the role of mother to Mary Jane and me, but disciplinarian as well, in a household where the father was home only on weekends. Although I continued to speak, I also "heard" something Dad had once told me, something that had never registered before: that it was our stepmother who had insisted on waiting three years before having children of her own, to give Mary Jane and me that long to have her to ourselves.

I went on talking, about the heavenly city and how I longed to see it closer. But what I was understanding for the first time was how threatened Mama Dabney had been by Dad's new marriage. Why she had reminded me so often that Mary Skeen was not my real mother. I recalled my teenage withdrawal, my sulks and hostility, but now I was seeing the heartache they had caused to the loving woman sitting in front of me.

When I finished my story we were both silent for a long time. "George," Mother whispered at last, "God has entrusted you with enormous truths."

He's doing it still, I thought! Even as I talked about the absolute acceptance I had encountered in Him, a brand new ability to accept Mother for herself was born in me.

What was the mysterious power in simply telling about this experience? I had wondered what God expected of me after such an encounter. Was this part of the answer? Just . . . to talk about it?

XI

But if my homecoming was even better than I hoped, starting med school the next day was worse. I was more than a month behind the rest of the class; the pile of books they loaded me down with, I could hardly carry back to the house, let alone hope to read and comprehend. In the lecture sessions that week the professors tossed out ten-syllable Latin words. All around me students were busy scribbling into notebooks while I was simply trying to understand what the topic was.

My health worked against me too. Simply walking between buildings on the campus left me exhausted, and concentrating on a lecture for more than a few minutes was impossible. Time after time in the evenings my head would snap erect and I'd realize I had been sleeping at my desk.

Each first-year student had been given an ordinary brown paper bag containing an assortment of human bones—rib, vertebra, ulna and radius—with which he was supposed to become familiar. One day I misplaced mine and anxiously retraced my steps to the anatomy lab. "Have you seen a bag of bones?" I asked a student standing in the doorway.

He surveyed my emaciated form. "Sure, Bud. Standing in front of me."

Gradually I slid into a destructive cycle. Worry ate into my study time. Then I did poorly and worried even more. The others all seemed so secure, so confident of their facts. As the weeks passed I began to feel like a lone moron surrounded by geniuses.

And then in May something wonderful happened.

I had known Marguerite Shell for a couple of years, ever since her brother Bob joined the Phi Gams at the University of Richmond. Bob Shell quickly became my best friend and I had first met Marguerite at his home in Lawrenceville, a small town about 70 miles south of Richmond. A petite brown-haired girl with blue eyes the color of the sky on an April morning, I thought Marguerite Shell was the most beautiful girl I'd ever seen. But as for dating her, I knew I didn't stand a chance. She was extremely popular; in fact soon after we met she was pinned to another fraternity brother of mine.

Bob Shell was now in the Navy V-12 program at the University of Richmond; one night he phoned with some news: Marguerite and her boyfriend had split up.

That was a surprise, but an even greater one was when I telephoned her for a date and she said yes. Gasoline was a problem with wartime rationing, but I talked Mama Dabney into loaning me her aqua-colored Oldsmobile and enough gas coupons for the round trip to Lawrenceville. That 1941 Oldsmobile was one of the prettiest cars ever made, with its streamlined shape and chrome-ringed radiator, and I thought I made a pretty dashing sight as I pulled into the Shells' driveway.

My self esteem was somewhat flattened when Marguerite looked over my shoulder toward the car door and asked, "Where's Bob?" But though she had obviously been expecting both of us, she came out with me anyway and we had a wonderful evening. After that my spare time was spent begging eight-hour passes from med school and gasoline coupons from the family.

By midsummer I knew that more than I'd ever wanted anything I wanted Marguerite to be my wife. I also knew I couldn't ask anyone to marry me without knowing about the most important event of my life, so several times I tried stumblingly to describe to Marguerite what had happened in the Barkeley hospital. Each time I saw the sparkle die out of her face and her blue eyes grow anxious, and I'd hastily change the subject. It was clear that she regarded the whole matter as a mental delusion. Anyhow, like many couples during the war we tried to keep things pretty much on the surface, instinctively shying away from the subject of death and the future.

And then in August I was summoned to appear before one of the school's administrators. In his airless small room he told me that unless I made a *B* in both biochemistry and bacteriology at the end of the current marking period, I would be returned immediately to active duty. He said a lot more, uncomplimentary reflections on the dimensions of my brain and the mental incompetence of whoever had admitted me to the program, while I stood at attention in the three feet between the door and his desk, feeling the last shreds of self-confidence desert me.

I was too wrapped up in my own problems to recognize that this man turned the same sarcastic tongue on all the students, part of a calculated strategy, no doubt, to winnow out before they reached the front as field doctors, all but the tough and self-reliant. To me his assessment was simply the confirmation of my own: I was too dumb to be a doctor.

For the next six weeks as I bent over textbooks and microscopes, his words played like a broken record in my head. My final grades in the two subjects were *D* and *E*.

On September 25 I was called again to his office. His first words were crisp and official. Reassignment to Camp Barkeley, effective immediately. Reclassification for active duty overseas, also effective as of this date. Then he added a personal note:

"Ritchie, if you get back from this war alive, I personally am going to see to it that you never get admitted into this medical school or any other. You've wasted the time of professors and staff, and you've kept out of the program a student who could have benefitted from such an opportunity. I'm going to see that you never again squander the time and resources of the medical profession."

I don't remember how I got out into the hallway. I only remember watching busy people passing briskly in front of me, people with places they had to be, and realizing that whether I walked to the right or to the left, up the stairs or down, it would not make the slightest difference to anyone on earth. It was the bleakest day of my life.

It was also my twenty-first birthday.

On the day when life was supposed to begin, mine had lost its purpose. What was there left but to go back to drilling in the Texas dust, and eventually to walk into a bullet somewhere in Europe or Asia. Why, Jesus, I kept asking. Why couldn't I have stayed with You in the first place?

The worst of it was, Mother was planning a big "surprise" party for me that night. Marguerite, who was working then in Richmond, was coming. My sister Mary Jane—her husband was in the Pacific—would be there, and Marguerite's older sister and her husband, and lots of others. And there would be gifts and congratulations and cards full of good wishes for the future.

I walked slowly to my locker, and took as long as I could about emptying it. Medical texts, notebooks full of ink-stained pages, my bag of bones. How could I ask Marguerite to marry me now, when I'd have no way to support her after the war—even supposing I got back?

How easy it would be, the thought came, to go up to the chemistry lab and mix a few ingredients in a beaker. . . . I might be too stupid to be a doctor, but I had understood the lectures on poisons well enough, and I wouldn't be the first ex-med student to take this way out.

The picture was in my mind for only an instant, crowded out by another one. The suicides I had seen chained for how long in a realm where a minute could last an eternity, to the very situations they had tried to escape. If I couldn't face Marguerite's disappointment in me that night, how could I bear it for a timeless forever? I saw those tortured eyes, heard their "I'm sorry!" endlessly repeated, never reaching the ears it was meant for, and I knew they would stand forever between me and any serious impulse to take my own life.

I went to my birthday party. I blew out the candles on my

cake, upwrapped ribbon and tissue paper, and laughed at the jokes about how much money doctors made. Then when the others were gone I told Mother and Marguerite.

They were wonderful about it, reminding me that a quarter of the class was always eliminated by that time. If not me, Marguerite pointed out, someone else would be feeling disappointment. Which only made me feel worse about the girl I was saying goodbye to.

"Immediately" in Army parlance meant of course "after an indefinite delay," so it was nearly three weeks before my orders came through to report back to Camp Barkeley. I left early one October morning with three other med students who like me had failed to stay in the program. One of the fellows had a car, an old black Plymouth, and we had arranged to drive out together.

We were a pretty silent group driving west through the glorious autumn colors. I kept thinking about Dad, somewhere in France. The great D-day invasion had taken place four months before, and Dad's unit had followed the first forces from the beachheads deep into France. It was during this advance that Dad's great contribution to the war had come. As they retreated, the Germans had had to abandon one of the great natural resources of Europe: the peat bogs of France and Belgium, vast natural reservoirs of fuel. To prevent this wealth from falling into allied hands, the retreating Germans systematically flooded the low-lying bogs, rendering them, most people believed, unusable for many years.

The problem was handed to Dad: within six weeks he had the peat works operational. Dad was a hero, his name mentioned in news stories and official reports.

And his son? Heading out to boot camp, exactly where ne was thirteen months before.

The only bright spot on my horizon that sparkling October day was a letter which had come from France the week before, hinting that Dad might be home by Christmas. Home! The family together! Except . . . by Christmas where would I be?

We got as far as Cincinnati that first night, not talking much, each of us probably wrestling with thoughts about like mine. By the next day we relaxed a little, taking turns at the wheel, talking about our girlfriends, the World Series, the fishing we'd done or hadn't done over the summer—everything except med school and the war.

Louisville, Memphis. The afternoon of the third day we reached the Mississippi and drove south along the east bank heading for the river crossing at Vicksburg. On both sides of the river stretched empty corn and sugar fields, miles and miles of brown stubble in the fall sunshine, ahead of us Vicksburg, Mississippi, on its high plateau. Pete was at the wheel, the rest of us watching for signs to the bridge which showed on our map.

In the city Pete took a street leading down toward the river. "See any signs?" he asked me over his shoulder. From my position in the back seat I was supposed to keep an eye out the left-hand window.

I didn't answer. For the last mile my mouth had been feeling dry, my stomach tight. Something about the layout of this town seemed strangely, impossibly, familiar:

I knew I had never been there before, and yet I knew exactly how the shoreline would look around the next curve. How the streets would intersect. There! Just as I'd known they would! And all at once I knew for sure that straight ahead on that very street we would come in a few blocks to a white frame building with a red roof and the word "Cafe" in neon letters over the door.

"There it is! To the left!" The guy in the front next to Pete pointed to a small sign at the corner. "The bridge must be back up that way."

Pete slowed the car and put out his hand to signal a left-hand turn.

"Please!" My voice was harsh. "Don't stop, Pete! Keep going straight."

The guy who had seen the sign turned around to stare at me. "The sign points up that way."

"I know. I—I'd just like to drive another couple of blocks in this direction, that's all."

Everyone in the car was looking at me now. "I thought I recognized something," I said.

Pete shrugged and straightened the wheel. "How much farther?" he said, driving slowly ahead.

My heart was hammering too hard to speak. A block ahead, on my side of the car, on the corner, was a white all-night cafe with a red roof. The neon letters over the door were turned off in the bright daylight but the Pabst sign was still propped in the right-hand window.

There was the sidewalk where I walked beside a man who could not see me. There was the telephone pole where I had stood so long . . . how long? In what kind of time and what kind of body?

"Stop!" I cried. For Pete was passing the little restaurant.

Pete pulled over to the curb and again I was aware of the stares of the others. It was a perfectly ordinary street, like a dozen others we had driven down since leaving Richmond.

"I thought you'd never been in Mississippi?" Pete said.

My hand was sweaty on the door handle. I longed to leap out of that car, to run across the street to that phone pole, to grab that guy wire, grab it and shake it. To open the door to that cafe and walk in and watch whoever was in there look up. To ask a question. What time is it? Anything, just to hear my own voice and hear them answer.

I let go of the handle and forced my eyes away from the white cafe on the corner. "I didn't think I had, either," I said.

What else could I say? I was here one night when I was also lying in a hospital bed in Texas?

Pete twisted the wheel impatiently and followed the signs back up the sloping streets to the bridge. But on the map on my lap my finger traced a line: Abilene, Texas—across Arkansas—across Louisiana . . . a straight line due east from Abilene to Vicksburg, Mississippi. As we drove across the broad brown expanse of water a voice inside me was shouting,

So it was here! Vicksburg, Mississippi. Here was where I stopped in that headlong bodiless flight. Here I stopped, and thought, and turned back. . . .

XII

I stayed only two weeks, this time, at Camp Barkeley. The soldiers I had trained with were gone, of course, shipped to battlefronts all over the world, and other trainloads of recruits had come and gone since then. Because of my partial medical training I was assigned to the Medical Administrative Corps and put in a holding company waiting assignment to a field hospital. Meanwhile the routine at Camp Barkeley was the same as for everyone else: marching, ten hours a day, in the eye-stinging, throat-clogging dust.

On my first time off I hitched a ride over to the hospital and looked up Lieutenant Irvine. "Bad break," she said when I told her about my poor performance in med school. "You weren't really back to normal, you know, when you left here. You'll do better next time, after the war."

She seemed so full of confidence in me that I didn't tell her what the school official had said. I wished I could tell her, though, about driving through Vicksburg and seeing a cafe where I had stood while my physical body lay in that very hospital ward. But my disastrous attempts to describe the experience to Marguerite had taught me something. Talking about the events of that night had a strange power —a power God could use. But it must be at His timing, as it had been with Mother, in our living room, the night I returned to Richmond. It was not something I could simply take on myself to talk about for reasons of my own. Then, as I had with Marguerite, I'd make a total mess of it.

In early November I was sent to Camp Rucker, Alabama, for training as a medical and surgical technician with the 123rd Evacuation Hospital. The Battle of the Bulge was underway in Europe, and units like the 123rd were being assembled and shipped to the front as rapidly as personnel could be found. I got only one weekend pass, just before Thanksgiving, for a swift trip from Alabama to Virginia and a brief visit with Marguerite and my family. Mother still expected Dad home by Christmas, and now all my hopes centered on seeing him before I myself sailed for France.

The 123rd boarded the train at Camp Rucker on Christmas Eve, 1944, bound for Camp Kilmer, New Jersey, and embarkation. That night, trying to sleep in the upright seat, my thoughts kept going back to the previous Christmas Eve when I awoke in a hospital bed with a pain in my chest and a memory of the most loving Presence I had ever known.

Where had He been in the year since then, this Jesus I had met? He could not have changed or gone away—that Light was too all-penetrating for me to imagine any time or place that He did not fill. But that, now, was simply head knowledge. Why wasn't He making more difference to the way I handled things? You'd expect, I told myself, that anyone who had had an experience like mine, anyone who had glimpsed even dimly the Love behind the universe, would no longer get upset by external things that happened.

But I was. Terribly. I was riled by the blustering sergeant sitting three seats ahead of me now, the smell of his black cheroot filling the coach. I was bothered when the men in the 123rd, mostly Northerners from big cities, made fun of my Southern accent and smalltown ideas. Instead of being able, now, to shrug such things off, I found them bothering me more than they ever had.

Toward morning the train stood for a long time on a dark stretch of tracks somewhere. There was a road nearby; occasionally I saw car headlights crossing an overpass up ahead. Then a wintry dawn broke and a great lump came into my throat. We were at the Acca switchyards just outside Richmond, Virginia, less than one mile from my home! There was the engine house of the old Richmond, Fredericksburg, and Potomac Railroad, where Papa Dabney used to bring me down to watch the trains. And that bridge! I must have pedalled my bicycle a thousand times over that road between my folks' place and Moss Side.

It was Christmas morning and my family was just one mile on the other side of those trees. The homesickness I had been fighting down rose up in a flood. I wondered if Henry and Bruce Gordon were awake yet—they were always the first ones up on Christmas morning. Had Dad gotten home yesterday? After being separated by thousands of miles and a world war, were we within a mile of each other at this moment?

About 7:00 A.M. there was a jerk and a grinding of wheels and the train began to move again. Speeding up, slowing, stopping, it took all day to reach Camp Kilmer, the longest Christmas of my life.

From a phone booth, somewhere in the camp, I talked to my family. Dad had been home; he had reached Richmond on Christmas Eve. Our sailing date was not known, of course, but they were issuing twelve-hour passes for the 28th. That wasn't time enough to get down to Richmond, but I could make it as far as Washington and back.

And so the family took a train from Richmond up to Washington, and I took one down from New Jersey. I saw them standing on the platform at Washington's Union Station before my coach even came to a stop, though it was a moment before I recognized the grey-haired man standing next to Mother. When he left for Europe Dad's hair had been jet black. His hair and the lines in his face spoke of what he had been through; he himself talked only of cheerful things—how good his family looked, how much I was going to enjoy the beautiful countryside of France. We had half an hour, sitting on a bench in the crowded waiting room. Then my return train was called and I waved from the window until I lost them in the crowd of other wartime farewells.

XIII

The 123rd Evac Hospital boarded the SS Brazil on New Year's Day, 1945, while the Red Cross dispensed doughnuts on the pier and a band played "My Mama Done Tol' Me." Three days out, the convoy was struck by a savage North Atlantic storm. The 123rd was berthed on the highest deck on the ship, just below the Captain's bridge, but high as we were, for two days waves smacked against the deck-houses and seeped under doorways. Under these conditions hard-boiled eggs seemed to be the only food the galleys could send up, but most of us were too seasick to eat anyway.

In spite of the storm there were apparently submarines in the area. For tension-wracked hours we sat on our crazily rocking bunks, stacked four high one above the other, listening to the depth charges drop from the lower decks and explode in the water far beneath us. Looking at the strained faces around me I realized two things about my own feelings. About the prospect of being torpedoed and having to take to lifeboats in that icy gale, I was as terrified as the next guy. The mechanics of dying, the pain and panic, were as frightening to me as they had ever been.

But as for death itself, I not only felt no fear of it, I found myself wishing it would happen. Then I would be with Him! I'd be out of this miserable world where men crossed an ocean to kill other men and where even among ourselves there was so little love.

At 4:00 A.M. on January 16th the SS Brazil anchored in a thick fog outside the French port of Le Havre. As it grew light we crowded the railings to catch our first look at Europe. Slowly the grey mist lifted: twisted steel hulks that had once been ships, a single wall where a block of buildings had stood—no newsreel had prepared me for my first view of a bombed-out city.

The harbor was too choked with wreckage for our ship to get closer and we were brought ashore in small landing craft, then marched to a row of open trucks for transport to Camp Lucky Strike, a staging point some sixty miles inland. The two-inch snowfall in the back of the trucks swiftly turned to ice as we trampled it with our boots. Most of the soldiers crouched down by the sides of the truck to get out of the piercing wind but I stood transfixed as we lumbered through the city, past gutted homes where shreds of bright wallpaper fluttered in the wind. I kept thinking of Dad with his lined face and grey hair, understanding better what the invasion had been like.

At Lucky Strike we put up our tents and then sat on our cots trying to rub some feeling back into our feet. We were

105

standing in the chow line the next morning when a jeep tore into the camp, the driver shouting something about a train wreck. We piled into every available vehicle and on the way got fragments of the story. It was American troops from our own SS Brazil who were aboard the train; sabotage by Vichy French forces was suspected.

Apparently our unit, on the highest deck, had been the first to be debarked from the ship and the only one to be sent on to Camp Lucky Strike by road. The entire rest of the ship, several thousand troops, had been loaded throughout the day and the evening onto a train of "forty and eight's," small French baggage cars built to carry either forty men or eight horses. It was after midnight before they were all aboard and the slow trip over the disrupted French rail system began. Approaching the nearby station of St.-Valery-en-Caux the train was mysteriously switched to a little-used side track terminating at the station house. Travelling full speed the train crashed into the brick wall of the building.

I had never seen or imagined such a scene of carnage. Some of the men had been killed outright, many more were pinned inside the wreckage crying out for help. We stepped over severed arms and legs, we wrestled with tangled metal keeping us from reaching our shipmates. I found myself assigned to a captain working in an improvised first-aid tent. But our medical supplies were not yet unloaded from the ship; for a long time between the doctor and me we had one pair of nurse's bandage scissors, a needle and thread, and a few emergency shots of morphine.

It was my first exposure to human suffering on a large scale. I had once thought I wanted to help people in pain. But I had been thinking of natural problems like Papa

106

Dabney and his arthritis. What was facing us today was suffering deliberately inflicted by one group of people on another. If hatred could grow this powerful—for we were preparing to do the same thing to them—who wanted to live in such a world?

At the end of the nightmare day, when the last casualty had been sent by ambulance to the nearest hospital, I found myself brooding on the fact that others had been permitted to leave this existence while I was condemned to stay. I had seen fellows my age die that day, and except for their suffering, felt a pang of envy for them. Why had our unit been the only one which was not aboard that train?

The question came back to torment me over and over in the weeks that followed, as time after time I found myself a few tents, a few yards, a few feet away from the leap into His presence we bodily creatures call death. From Camp Lucky Strike the 123rd Evac traveled to Rethel, France, three hundred and fifty miles east, where we could service troops from the combat zones. We set up our tent city—hospital, sleeping quarters, mess—on the grounds of an abandoned chateau, its tall windows broken and dark, weeds growing in the circular driveway.

And there as we cared for the injured and dying, my longing for death became an obsession. I saw the fact of physical survival as a judgment on me, a rejection of me by the Person whose love meant everything.

✗ I was sitting on a tree stump behind the chateau one afternoon, asking again to be allowed into His presence, when a master sergeant came running through the yard. "On your feet, soldier!" he barked. "An Air Force sergeant's in C-tent with his knee darn near blown away."

Inside C-tent I spotted him right away: an Air Force

107

jacket lay on the foot locker and when I saw it my whole body went tense. Three stripes above, three stripes below, a diamond in the middle: the guy wasn't only a sergeant, he was a top sergeant, and every top sergeant I'd known was a foul-mouthed, small minded, bullying—

"Hi! My name's Jack Helms. What's yours?"

Looking up from the cot through eyes glazed with pain and morphine was a fellow around my own age. He was obviously hurting badly, but when I had told him my name he wanted to know a lot of other things about me, where I was from, what kinds of things I liked to do, did I have brothers and sisters. Talking helped keep his mind off the pain, he said.

In spite of myself, as I changed his dressing, I found myself asking him questions too. He told me he was from El Dorado, Arkansas, that he had been working as a car hop in a restaurant there. That morning the Jeep he'd been driving had hit a land mine; luckily his had been the only injury.

A doctor came in to examine the injury and give me instructions for keeping it clean. When I had done what he told me there was no reason to stay, but I kept hanging around the bed. There was something about Jack—he didn't like to be called "Sergeant"—that made you want to be near him. He reminded me of somebody, but I couldn't think who. He was a big good-looking fellow with a deeply tanned face and dark brown eyes, but it was his smile that was unforgettable. It split his face from ear to ear and enveloped you and the big green tent and the whole muddy evac hospital in a glow of appreciation.

I had treated knee injuries before and I knew they kept on being painful. But Jack never mentioned this; he seemed more concerned about my problems than his own. When he heard about the med school fiasco he was on fire with eagerness for me to go back, after the war, and try again. All he would talk about was my great future as a doctor.

When I told him about the guy who was going to keep me out of school, he broke into one of his sunburst smiles. "People say a lot of things. If my guess is right, he won't even be at that school when you get back."

As a medical tech my job included everything from carrying trays and bedpans to giving shots and running errands to the PX. Like the other techs I had pretty much been putting in time until my shift was over. Now to my surprise I found myself staying late, working extra hours. Who was it Jack reminded me of, and why did I feel so good when I was with him?

I was curious, his second day in the hospital, when an Air Force major showed up asking for Sergeant Helms. In the rigid caste systems of the services, officers and enlisted men had little off-duty contact. When I led him to C-tent, however, the major sat down at the foot of Jack's cot and chatted for half an hour. Jack told me later that this was the officer he had been driving when their Jeep hit the mine and overturned. "So it's natural that he would feel concerned about me."

Already I was discovering that behavior that was "natural" around Jack was somehow different from ordinary behavior. To me the most remarkable part of the major's continuing visits was not the greeting Jack gave him, but that he gave the same greeting to anyone who stopped to talk to him . . . including me. Jack seemed to make no distinction between the major or the surgeon who operated on his knee, and the lowly tech who changed his bed sheets.

Within a week Jack was hobbling about in a cast, and now whenever I wasn't on duty we'd take a walk together, at first just around the grounds of the chateau, picking our way through the weeds of what had once been a sunken garden, then out along the road which led to Rethel. Ostensibly I was helping a wounded airman make a recovery. But I was aware, and I suspected Jack was too, that the greater healing was taking place in me.

We talked about everything on those walks, school, childhood, careers, and all the time the feeling grew that I had known Jack Helms before. He was a deeply committed Christian, I learned, a Protestant, although he attended church with the Catholic family who had adopted him and shown him great kindness. And all at once one day, without intending to any more than I had intended talking to my stepmother, I found myself telling him about the night I had come out of a hospital movie theater and asked a ward boy for some aspirin. As they had been the earlier time, the words were simply there. I told him all of it: the ambulance ride to the X-ray section, waking up in a strange small room to find someone else in my bed, walking down a street in Vicksburg, Mississippi, trying to get a passerby to listen to me.

It was the second time I had been able to talk about my experience. I could tell by the wonderment in Jack's face that he had never heard anything even remotely like what I was describing. I could also see by his expression that not for an instant did he doubt what I was saying. I described the Light that had entered the little cubicle. How my whole life had somehow entered at the same time, lit up by a love such as I had never . . .

I stopped, staring at Jack. That nagging feeling that I

had known him before. That strange sense I'd had the very first day of being in the presence of a familiar friend . . .

It was Christ who all this time had been looking at me out of Jack Helms' eyes.

The acceptance. The caring. The joy. Of course I recognized these things! I had encountered them in a hospital room in Texas, and now, five thousand miles away, I had met them again on a hillside in France. They were echoes only, this time, imperfect, transmitted through a fallible human being. But at least I knew now from Whom the message was coming.

So much was falling into place as we turned around on the road and headed back toward camp. For once neither of us spoke. Jack did not press me to continue my interrupted story; he seemed in his perceptive way to know that I was working something out in my mind.

The lonesomeness I had felt that year, the alienation from the world and the things that went on here, wasn't it all a longing to go back to the time when I had stood in His presence? But could you ever find Him, I wondered as we crested a hill, by going backwards? The very nature of the Person I had met was His now-ness. He was overwhelmingly and everywhere Present, so that no other time could even exist where He was. It was no good, I suddenly saw, looking for Him in the past, even when that past was only fifteen months before. I knew that afternoon, on the road from Rethel, that if I wanted to feel the nearness of Christ—and I did want that, above everything else—I would have to find it in the people that He put before me each day.

We had reached the chateau grounds as these thoughts went whirling through my head. We walked around in back; there was the tree stump on which I had sat, only a little over two weeks before, praying to be allowed to die. And all at once I knew something else, on this day of new insights.

That prayer had been answered.

In a sense in which I never meant it, I had indeed died. For the first time in many months I had put aside my self-pity, my self-incrimination—all thoughts of any kind about myself—long enough to get involved with someone else. Jack's injury and his healing had been the one thing on my mind those last two weeks; in caring for him I had lost sight of myself.

And in losing myself, I had discovered Christ. It was strange, I thought: I'd had to die, in Texas, too, to see Him. I wondered if we always had to die, some stubborn part of us, before we could see more of Him.

Jack stayed only another week in the hospital before returning to his air base, but in that week we cemented a friendship that has lasted thirty years. Because he lives today in Malibu Beach, California, and I in Charlottesville, Virginia, we don't see each other often, but every visit picks up as though we had just strolled off a country road in France.

That was the beginning, for me, that country walk, the moment when I began to integrate the near-death experience in Barkeley, Texas, with all the rest of my life. The first step, I realized, was to stop trying to recapture that otherworldly vision of Jesus, and start looking for him in the faces across the mess table. x

That wasn't easy for a young soldier who had spent all his life in a small southern city. Roman Catholics, Jews, Negroes —I had grown up believing these people were not only different from me, but not as good. And so Jesus in His mercy had put me in the 123rd Evac. He let me start with Jack because Jack was easy; you had to see the Christ in Jack. But before long I started seeing Jesus in a Jew from New York, an Italian from Chicago, a black from Trenton.

I discovered something else and at first it puzzled me. The more I learned to see Christ in other people, the less I was crushed by the death and suffering our unit dealt with. It seemed like it would be the opposite, the more you found to love in people, the harder it would be to see their pain. It never got easy, of course, but it became somehow . . . bearable, and again I found myself thinking back to the Texas experience.

I had been glamorizing that memory, I realized, dwelling only on the joy of His presence. But when I recalled it honestly, there had been much in that "other realm" that was frankly hideous, scenes of agony worse than anything even in the train wreck at St.-Valery. I had told myself I wanted to leave this earth because I had seen a better place. But that wasn't true I began to realize: the afterworld I had glimpsed was both infinitely brighter than this one, and infinitely more savage and terrible. Why hadn't the evil side of that world crushed my spirit—as the negatives of this world had done?

I had started reading the Bible, back in my tent, and one day I came to a Psalm that seemed to help. "If I ascend to heaven," I read in Psalm 139, "thou art there! If I make my bed in Sheol, thou art there!" Of course, that was the answer: Jesus had been there, in those scenes of Sheol. It was His light, His compassion in which I was seeing the awfulness, and that shed a ray of hope, even in hell.

When the war in Europe ended in May 1945, the 123rd Evac entered Germany with the occupying troops. I was part

113

of a group assigned to a concentration camp near Wuppertal, charged with getting medical help to the newly liberated prisoners, many of them Jews from Holland, France, and eastern Europe. This was the most shattering experience I had yet had; I had been exposed many times by then to sudden death and injury, but to see the effects of slow starvation, to walk through those barracks where thousands of men had died a little bit at a time over a period of years, was a new kind of horror. For many it was an irreversible process: we lost scores each day in spite of all the medicine and food we could rush to them.

Now I needed my new insight indeed. When the ugliness became too great to handle I did what I had learned to do. I went from one end to the other of that barbed wire enclosure looking into men's faces until I saw looking back at me the face of Christ.

And that's how I came to know Wild Bill Cody. That wasn't his real name. His real name was seven unpronounceable syllables in Polish, but he had long drooping handlebar mustaches like pictures of the old western hero, so the American soldiers called him Wild Bill. He was one of the inmates of the concentration camp, but obviously he hadn't been there long: his posture was erect, his eyes bright, his energy indefatigable. Since he was fluent in English, French, German and Russian, as well as Polish, he became a kind of unofficial camp translator.

We came to him with all sorts of problems; the paper work alone was staggering in attempting to relocate people whose families, even whole hometowns, might have disappeared. But though Wild Bill worked fifteen and sixteen hours a day, he showed no signs of weariness. While the rest of us were drooping with fatigue, he seemed to gain strength.

"We have time for this old fellow," he'd say. "He's been waiting to see us all day." His compassion for his fellow-prisoners glowed on his face, and it was to this glow that I came when my own spirits were low.

So I was astonished to learn when Wild Bill's own papers came before us one day, that he had been in Wuppertal since 1939! For six years he had lived on the same starvation diet, slept in the same airless and disease-ridden barracks as everyone else, but without the least physical or mental deterioration.

Perhaps even more amazing, every group in the camp looked on him as a friend. He was the one to whom quarrels between inmates were brought for arbitration. Only after I'd been at Wuppertal a number of weeks did I realize what a rarity this was in a compound where the different nationalities of prisoners hated each other almost as much as they did the Germans.

As for Germans, feeling against them ran so high that in some of the camps liberated earlier, former prisoners had seized guns, run into the nearest village and simply shot the first Germans they saw. Part of our instructions were to prevent this kind of thing and again Wild Bill was our greatest asset, reasoning with the different groups, counseling forgiveness.

"It's not easy for some of them to forgive," I commented to him one day as we sat over mugs of tea in the processing center. "So many of them have lost members of their families."

Wild Bill leaned back in the upright chair and sipped at his drink. "We lived in the Jewish section of Warsaw," he began slowly, the first words I had heard him speak about himself, "my wife, our two daughters, and our three little boys. When the Germans reached our street they lined everyone against a wall and opened up with machine guns. I begged to be allowed to die with my family, but because I spoke German they put me in a work group."

He paused, perhaps seeing again his wife and five children. "I had to decide right then," he continued, "whether to let myself hate the soldiers who had done this. It was an easy decision, really. I was a lawyer. In my practice I had seen too often what hate could do to people's minds and bodies. Hate had just killed the six people who mattered most to me in the world. I decided then that I would spend the rest of my life—whether it was a few days or many years—loving every person I came in contact with."

Loving every person . . . this was the power that had kept a man well in the face of every privation. It was the Power I had first met in a hospital room in Texas, and was learning little by little to recognize wherever He chose to shine through—whether the human vehicle was aware of Him or not.

I returned to the States from occupation duty in Germany in the spring of 1946, and Marguerite and I were married the following year. When the moment came to tell her about the Texas experience, it happened, as it had the two previous times, naturally, almost effortlessly on my part, helping the love between us grow.

Meanwhile Jack Helms' hunch had proved correct; the administrator who had sworn to keep me out of there was no longer connected with the Medical College of Virginia. The man who went to bat to get me readmitted was Dr. Sidney Negus, the professor who had given me the *D* in biochemistry. This time I was determined not to make the mistake I had made before. My trouble began, I saw now, when I took my eyes off Jesus and onto myself. This time I didn't worry about my stupidity or my poor record, and I got through school without difficulty.

From the outset of my career, however, I discovered what all doctors know: medicine does not have all the answers. When stumped, as I often was, I would pray for my patient —silently, under my breath—asking Jesus' help in making the right diagnosis, prescribing the right treatment. In addition Marguerite and I formed the habit of praying together for patients every evening.

I continued to read the Bible. It was funny, in Sunday School the Bible had seemed to me both boring and difficult. Since Texas it had become simply a factual description of life. When Jesus said to some fishermen on a lakeside, "Follow me," of course they dropped everything and hurried after Him—who could resist? When He said "I am the Light of the world," it was simply an observable fact.

But if my experience made the Bible comprehensible, much more so, as I now began to read it systematically after the war, it was the Bible which helped me understand the experience. Reading over and over the accounts of the crucifixion, I understood at last where that certainty had come from, in His presence, that I was not condemned, in spite of the ugly actions I had committed which were paraded in plain view before us. It was His death, I came to see, that had already paid for these things, the light of His resurrection in which we stood.

Why these cosmic acts should have applied to me— whether I could somehow have appropriated them in that church service at age eleven?—I didn't know. But I began to understand, reading the Bible, how all-important our lives on this earth are, in His plan. How terribly wrong I had been, on the SS Brazil, at St.-Valery, in Rethel, to detest mine, to ask Him to take me out of this world before His work in me here was done.

I thought of the wretched souls I had seen in that first post-earthly realm, trapped in hatreds and lusts, fixed on material things forever out of reach. Somehow none of them had finished growing up in their time on earth, whether it had been long or short. I had no trouble believing that some of the teenagers I had seen blown to bits in Europe had accomplished already the goals God had for them on earth, were well prepared to graduate to some sphere nearer Him. But I certainly had not been. With my self-centeredness, my prejudices, my self-righteousness—how had I dared ask to die! In yearning for Jesus had I forgotten what He showed me? That plain crawling with the unhappiest beings I had ever seen, each insisting on his own superiority to the annihilation of everybody else . . . had I seriously wanted an eternity in some existence like that? Would I ever, in fact, reach the point where I'd be willing to say, on my own, I've done what I'm supposed to do on earth?

XIV

One winter evening in 1952—it was around the middle of December because we had just had our annual Christmas party at the Richmond Academy of Medicine which I had recently joined—I sat in the living room reading a copy of *Life* magazine. The issue was full of ads for brand name turkeys and hams, with jolly Santas on every other page, and I was flipping through it without much interest when suddenly my fingers tightened.

On the page in front of me was a drawing of a gigantic sphere-shaped structure cut away to reveal men and machines inside it. There was a kind of traveling crane mounted on steel girders, turbines, a huge circular tank, stairs, catwalks, down in one corner a small control room.

What set my heart pounding in my throat was not the

strange futuristic appearance of these objects but the certainty that I had seen all this before. Not recently, either. Somehow, years ago, I had stood staring not at a drawing of this enormous sphere but at the thing itself. I had wandered about that peculiar interior too; I had seen the stairway just there, peered into that vast tank of water.

But . . . I couldn't have! Skimming the text I saw that what I remembered was impossible:

Last week the Atomic Energy Commission partially lifted its veil of secrecy and allowed Life's artists to make a drawing of some details of the prototype of the second US atomic submarine engine and the strange house that holds it. The building, now going up near Schenectady, N.Y., will be the world's largest man-made sphere, a $2-million, two hundred and twenty-five foot steel shell.

The article went on to say that to avoid possible radioactive contamination scientists would build the submarine engine inside the sphere, then submerge it for tests in the giant tank. Baffled, I lowered the magazine to my lap. I had felt so certain I'd seen this whole operation, yet I had never been to Schenectady. Anyhow, what I recalled was some time ago and this was just now being built. The thing I had seen was finished and operating, though I hadn't had any idea what—

Then I remembered. It was in that tranquil campus-like realm inhabited by beings wrapped in thought as monks are wrapped in robes, that I had stood in 1943 as the earth measures times, staring at a huge sphere-shaped building, walking through its intricate fittings. . . .

What was that realm? In what mysterious way was it related to the life and thought of the world where I sat in 1952, with Marguerite talking on the telephone in the hall and Christmas cards lining the mantlepiece? I did not think about it very long, except to wonder if philosophers are right when they say that certain ideas seem to drop into widely scattered areas of the world from "somewhere" simultaneously. I had grown wary of inquiring into super-terrestrial areas on my own. As long as Christ had been my guide, there had been nothing to fear. But since my out-of-the-body experience—nine years before—I had come across individuals who had become so fascinated by the "spirit" world that they seemed to have lost sight of the Spirit Himself.

All I was sure of as I sat in the living room that evening was that the time had come to start talking far more publicly than I had until then about my encounter with Christ. If we were truly entering the age of atomic power, without knowing the Power which created it, then it was only a matter of decades until we destroyed ourselves and our earth as well. It wasn't enough for professional clergy to speak out; everyone who had any experience at all of God, it seemed to me, had a responsibility. And it must again have been His timing: I who could never string two words together found myself talking to youth groups, clubs, churches, anyone who would listen to the message that God is love, and all else is hell.

Professionally, of course, I was sure this meant the ruin of me, and doubtless I did lose some patients who weren't willing to entrust themselves to a "religious fanatic." But it was odd, the people whose scorn I feared most were often the most accepting. When I applied for my residency in psychiatry at the University of Virginia Hospital I was advised by a friend on the staff not to mention my experience since he didn't know how the others might take this. The very first person to interview me turned out to be Dr. Wilfred Abse, Professor of Psychoanalysis and Analytical Psychotherapy in the Department of Psychiatry, and one of the top men in the Virginia Psychoanalytic Society.

I had no sooner stepped into his office than Dr. Abse confronted me with, "Well, Dr. Ritchie, I understand that you feel that you have met the Christ." I saw my chances at the University of Virginia floating out the window. Dr. Abse was a Jew, a Freudian analyst, and he was asking me a direct question which demanded an answer. Under my breath, as I had done so often, I turned to Jesus: "Lord, what do I say now?"

Deny me before man, the words seemed almost audible, *and I will deny you before my Father.*

To Dr. Abse I said, "I can no more deny the reality of what happened to me in Barkeley, Texas, than Saul of Tarsus could deny what happened to him on the road to Damascus."

And that was that, I thought, for my chances of becoming a psychiatrist. Imagine my surprise, a couple of weeks later, to receive a letter telling me that I had been accepted unanimously by the examining staff. Years later, when Dr. Abse and I had become good friends, he told me that that particular conversation had been critical indeed. "All of us up here knew that you claimed to have had an out-of-the-body experience. If you'd pretended with me even for a moment that it hadn't happened, I'd have put you down as a deeply insecure person, and most probably an emotionally disturbed one who couldn't distinguish between fact and fancy."

In the consulting room itself, of course, in keeping with sound psychiatric practice, I seldom mention my personal views of God. Only where the need is extreme, as with Fred Owen, do I violate that professional silence.

"Do you know why I come to the office early each morning?" I asked him one day when we were discussing the effects in my life of the Texas experience. "Before the other doctors and staff get here? It's because I use that time to pray for each of the patients I will see that day. I believe Jesus has an agenda and a timetable for each of us, and I pray that with His help the patient and I may discover it together."

If Jesus was giving Fred Owen only weeks on earth instead of decades, "it's because He knows you can finish your work here in weeks. You can forgive and receive forgiveness. You can free yourself of addictions and angers—any baggage you don't want to carry into a realm where everything is Light."

I do not know of course what went on in the innermost recesses of Fred Owen's heart; psychiatry at best is limited by what the patient shares with us. I do know that the man who came into my office on May 9, 1977, for what turned out to be our final session, was a very different person from the man I had first seen in December. Physically he was weaker of course. In fact a neighbor had to drive him, and he lay on the yellow sofa throughout the session. But the things he said between the labored breaths, and the peace—even humor—in his eyes, filled me with joy. He had been battling with his former employers to get his hospital bills included under their health plan; I had filled out a number of forms in the case myself. That week he had received final notification that his claim had been denied, on the grounds that he had quit work without the required notice.

"You know what?" he told me. "They're right. I quit

because I was mad and I wanted to make problems for them. Only now I'm the one with the problems."

He gave a laugh that was interrupted by a cough, but the sound was beautiful to me because it was a real laugh, a heart-laugh, without a trace of bitterness in it. "It's like what we were reading, right, doc? 'As you sow, so you reap.' If I've learned that in time, then losing the insurance was cheap.

"You know what I do now that I'm not sleeping so well at night?" he went on. "I pray for those guys at work— that the shop will have a real good year, more business and profits than they know what to do with."

No man, of course, may speculate on another man's experience beyond the grave, but when that same neighbor telephoned to tell me about Fred Owen's death on May 24, I had no trouble picturing, at least, that moment of astonished transition. The growing Light. The joy in the heart of a man who had done his homework well.

God is busy building a race of men who know how to love. I believe that the fate of the earth itself depends on the progress we make—and that the time now is very short. As for what we'll find in the next world, here too I believe that what we'll discover there depends on how well we get on with the business of loving, here and now.